**Leanna Conley** has been telling stories, either as a performer or a writer, for her entire life.

Starting her career at age 7, she played the role of Sneezy in Snow White and the Seven Dwarves, on the ABC Detroit affiliate WXYZ-TV. Later, in her twenties, she performed alongside Tim Meadows and Chris Farley on The Second City stage in Chicago.

She later moved to Manhattan, where she made appearances on the Syfy Channel, Comedy Central, in indie films and commercials, and off-Broadway theatres. Stand-up comedy has also always been one of her passions. She has been featured in the Broads of Broadway and Full Metal Mamas stand-up comedy troupes, and has hosted countless comedy shows all over New York City.

D1556956

# The Daily Janet

## Leanna Conley

### with

## Dave Smitherman

First published in 2016
© Leanna Conley and Dave Smitherman

The right of Leanna Conley to be identified as the author of this work
has been asserted.

This edition published in 2016 by Astor and Blue Editions LLC of
1330 Avenuse of the Americas, Suite 23A,
New York, New York, 10019, U.S.A.
www.houseofstratus.com

Typeset by Astor + Blue

A catalogue record for this book is available from the British Library
and the Library of Congress.

ISBN 168-120-904-7
EAN 978-168-120-904-3

This is a fictional work and all characters are drawn from the author's imagination.
Any resemblance or similarities to persons either living or dead are entirely coincidental.

# DEDICATION

For the One and Only

Janet

This book is homage to my mother: a fashionista and dreamer
who chain-smokes, drinks, swears like a sailor, and dresses like
Ava Gardner. She is the Mother to end all Mothers.
Yes, folks, she's little Janet Lee.

height 5 5½
weight 114
hair red
eyes green
bust 36
waist 23
hips 36
glove 6½
hat 21½
shoes 7½AA
dress 8-10

# THE EQUATION

Ava Gardner voguing on the dance floor with a bottle
of Budweiser
+
Joan Rivers interviewing celebrities on the red carpet
+
Lucille Ball mixed with a smidge of Zsa Zsa Gabor
=
JANET

# Prologue

## Manhattan, December 1993

It's thirty degrees, but feels like zero on $8^{th}$ Avenue and 39th Street, Midtown Manhattan, in front of the New York Comedy Club on open mic night. The neon sign is the warmest thing around for miles. In my bulky gloves, I'm trying to study my set list, a piece of paper standup comics refer to (usually nervously) before going on stage to do their "act." Incidentally, that's something I've never had...an act. There are so many unbelievably funny incidents in my life and so many ways to present my "persona" that I've had difficulty finding it. What I did discover, however, was that my childhood is a goldmine for comedy material, especially as it relates to the one and only Janet. I usually refer to her as "Janet" because "Mother" doesn't do her justice.

I move up in line and pay $5, the going rate here for stage time. Open mic consists of a strange mix of hopeful twenty-year-olds and jaded veteran comics attempting to hone their painful existence into something meaningful; i.e. "jokes," in a dark, musty building with an aroma of sweat and beer. It's often a failed experiment with blank, hostile stares from the comic-filled audience after each futile line is delivered, sailing through the air only to land in the cold New York dust of indifference.

"And now, all the way from Detroit, Michigan..." The emcee was rolling his eyes even before he turned his head to wave me up on stage. "...The Dark Yupster!"

Uh, yeah, "Dark Yupster;" I came up with that name figuring I did go to a private school—hence yuppie—and I needed an edge.

1

I didn't dare use my real name, Leanna Conley Trojan. It's why I've hid for most of my life. My regal, historically stately name was reduced, oh, sometime in 1901, to a condom factory punch line. As time went on and the comedy world got bluer, it was something I couldn't deny, least of all on stage.

"I can't protect you. I can only stretch so far…"

No laughs.

"My name is originally Trojanowicz. In Polish that means 'slow moving rubber…'"

Dead air punctured with a random cough to bring it home.

I eventually decided to drop the condom under the bed where it belongs, and although I regretted kicking my father's lineage by abandoning the surname that I loved, I became Leanna Conley. It was a good move. I got some good reviews in the local press, some comedy awards, and several TV pilots. Finally it seemed I might be catching up with my friends and acquaintances who "made it." Things were looking up. Until one chance evening in Uptown Manhattan, at Stand Up New York on 72nd Street off Broadway. And, yes, there were Comedy Central talent scouts in the audience.

"And," the crowd, all smartly citified and well-dressed was hanging on my every word, "he was a…"

"Do Kennedy!" A familiar female voice rang out and my mother Janet stood up in the crowd, her glittery black barrette and matching blazer cuffs unmistakable, her cigarette glowing eerily in the semi-darkness.

"Oh, we have a newcomer here. Waitress please!" I laughed.

"Newcomer? It's me, your mother!" she announced.

"That's news to me." Audience laughter.

"Please, darling, it brings the house down every Christmas when you do Kennedy in the living room," she pleaded.

"Jackie thought the same thing." More laughs.

It was obvious that she would not sit down until I "did Kennedy." So I started to imitate him, and it was flawless. Half the audience got the reference and the other half thought "Kennedy" was the 90s MTV VJ.

"Ask not what you can do for your country. Ask what your wife can do for the Kennedy boys on a three-Martini lunch!"

Janet literally laughed herself off her chair, and that made the audience roar. (Disclaimer: That Kennedy bit I got from friend who stole it from, I think, Jim Gaffigan so thanks, uh, to you both…it was an emergency situation.)

The wait staff righted Janet on her chair and we continued. She wanted me to play the Steinway piano that was situated behind me onstage. So I dramatically went over and pounced on the keys, à la Victor Borge, only to manage a simple rendition of Chopsticks. The crowd loved it and Janet, even more. I only wish Comedy Central had shared her enthusiasm.

"Brava, darling! Brava!" She clapped.

After a little more back-and-forth banter, the crowd cheered. By the end of my set we both took the stage and did a bow. Janet was beaming with pride as she soaked in the adulation.

As we got down off the stage, I was greeted by pats on the back to the tune of: "Great act" and "When are you both performing together again?"

"For the rest of our lives…apparently."

I can't say I was entirely pleased with how the show went. In fact, I was actually pissed. There she goes again, my little diva, taking the stage. I was wondering if I would ever measure up to her expectations or have any moment in the limelight that was just my own.

The next week I did my act again, this time without Janet, and I "killed" (a standup term for knocking it out of the park). Naturally, there were no talent scouts in the audience. However, what I did realize was that anytime I included stories from my childhood, especially ones that focused on my unique mother, the crowd really responded. There was an instant connection.

This was a pleasant turn of events because now, apparently I could use those embarrassing, strange, and sometimes even painful moments as grist for the comedy mill. Maybe I did have an act and a stage persona just like Rosanne, Ellen, or fellow Detroiter Tim Allen. To build my act, I just needed to relive some of those childhood experiences and find the funny (or a toolbox).

With some stories that was surprisingly easy, and with others, it was almost impossible. However, the more I let people into my world, the stronger the performer/audience connection became. Most people couldn't believe the stories were true, and they laughed even harder (perhaps with a tad of shock and sympathy) when they found out they were real.

With a childhood like mine, I didn't need an act or a persona, I just needed to take Janet to the doctor's office or record one of her calls with an AT&T customer service representative who she's telling her life story to. Or I could show up at Janet's doorstep with a good-looking salesman and see how fast she serves him a Martini along with her vampy antics!

There's no doubt in my mind that wherever we have gone, Janet and I have been a pretty strong act for a long, long time. And *that* definitely makes life worth living every day.

# Chapter 1: Simply Irresistible

*I haven't done this much pushing since I got my husband promoted to V.P. at the Ford dinner in Des Moines!*

I met Janet Lee on one of the most atypical days of her life. Normally, she lived for the hours she spent shopping, designing outfits she had made at the local shops, or showing off the latest fashions on the catwalk. She spent her down time prowling boutiques and department stores buying more treasures for her packed closet, sipping her favorite Stoli Martini, squeaky dry with three olives, or admiring her genetically blessed figure; sometimes she would do all of them at the same time! However, on this steamy August day in 1962 at a hospital just outside of Detroit, Michigan, Janet the fashion plate wasn't expecting a Chanel suit from her tailor or a delivery from Saks Fifth Avenue. Instead, she was making a delivery of her very own, one that weighed in at 6.2 pounds to be exact.

The times were a little unsettling, what with missiles being hidden under tarps in Cuba and Khrushchev pounding his shoe at the United States. To add to the national tension, it seemed that almost every hospital—like the one where I was born—served double duty as a bomb shelter. So even while families were experiencing one of the most joyful gifts that life has to offer, they were constantly being reminded that they could grab their slippery newborns and scurry off to the protective basement should the need arise. Despite these troubling times (or perhaps because of them), Americans everywhere threw themselves, heart and soul, into the media-generated fantasy of Camelot with its promise of culture and peace that would surely protect the country from outside harm. After all, the charismatic John F. Kennedy was President, and he was married to the beautiful Jackie. Sometimes that was all that really mattered.

Being quite the romantic herself, Janet was the quintessential JFK groupie. Jackie Kennedy was her idol, role model, and fashion inspiration. Janet had even framed a picture of the first family to bring with her to the delivery room. Of course she couldn't stop there. She even provided each of her nurses with white pillbox hats (that she made herself) to match their uniforms. I was just being born, so I've had to rely on my dear mother Janet and my father, an auto executive, for all the glorious details. I can't imagine what the hospital staff was thinking during all of this, but perhaps it offered them a bit of escape from their daily routines. I only wish I could have actually been able to take in the spectacle of it all, the sea of uniformed nurses with matching hats. It had the makings of a "Simply Irresistible" Robert Palmer '80s music video, the stunned models all in the same dresses trying to keep up with the mullet wearing, skinny-black-tied rock star, but not quite knowing what had hit them.

So while my father was in the lobby making bets with the other soon-to-be dads on whether I'd be a boy or a girl, Janet was being paid an interesting visit. A man in coveralls walked into her room, and I'm sure she was a bit groggy as she was waiting to be prepped for the delivery room.

"I'm here to shave you," he said bluntly.

Janet looked at him for a minute. "Who are you, the cleanup crew? I think that area is taken care of."

"Yes, I am the janitor," he said matter-of-factly.

"Oh," Janet slurred. "Well then go right ahead."

Apparently he did a nice job shaving Janet and even that didn't stop her zeal to hobnob with the doctor, nurses, anesthesiologist, orderlies… and the cleaning staff. She never saw that man again, but I'd like to thank him for making my exit just that much smoother. Little did I know that delivery would be the smoothest that my life was ever going to get.

Between contractions, Janet was definitely in her element chatting with the afternoon shift like they were old friends, sharing helpful hair and makeup tips, and of course paying tribute to Mrs. Kennedy. I'm sure it was great fun for the nurses to see this local celebrity soaking up the attention, as if the reason for her stay was secondary, which at the moment it was. Janet has always displayed impeccable taste and style, so naturally she had designed her own couture for this occasion in silk chiffon and satin. For my birth, her pregnancy gown and robe was crafted of stunning yellow silk with matching satin slippers, her hair and makeup star-quality. Her belief, then and now, is that every detail should be fashionable—even down to the mink sanitary napkin belt she wore, a present from her friends at the Royal Oak Civic theater group. She's a stickler for details and originality.

"Ah, Mrs. C, you couldn't uv!" exclaimed Juanita, Mom's petite nurse, admiring her new Jackie hat. "Choo are so glamorous! Now I yam, too."

"Darling, that hat should be standard issue for heaven's sake! And I'd take care of those eyebrows if I were you. Give 'em a whack." She sipped on the little silver flask of Manhattans that the nurses had smuggled in for her.

"Oh, thanks, Mrs. C...Now pooosh! Pooosh!" the nurses urged her on.

"I haven't done this much pushing since I got Bill promoted to VP at the Ford dinner in Des Moines!" The nurses all giggled.

"Ahh!" Janet screamed, clutching a Givenchy throw blanket to distract herself. "I'll be stretched to kingdom come. If I'm not fitting into my couture Valentino satin pants after this, someone's going to be sorry!" They giggled again with a few "oooooooohs" added in.

For nineteen hours I attempted to delay meeting the woman to whom I've dedicated this book. Instinctively, like Bette Davis said, I knew to fasten my seat belt because it was going to be a bumpy ride. Or should I say "a bumpy life?" That's why I held on inside that womb cocoon as tightly as I could for as long as I could. But Janet, drawing on a well of strength, gave a final push, and I was out.

All of a sudden, my little eyes fluttered open, and when I was lifted into the air, I apparently realized I had lungs because they say I opened my mouth and screamed. Everyone there, including the lovely nurses, seemed to think it was perfectly normal. However, they did not have the bird's eye view that I was afforded as I was dangled in front of my mother. On her day of labor, the perfectly made-up face of Janet, complete with heavy Chanel eyeliner and bright red lips, smiled at me, and I screamed again. I guess the spectacle of it all was just too much for me. I wasn't ready for all of that fabulousness, but I didn't have much choice.

From that point on, I was going to have a Janet-packed life whether I liked it or not. I had to learn fast that this train would be leaving with or without me so I'd better just jump on board, "*dahrrrling!*" Of course I'd have to look my best while doing it because by my side would be the most glamorous, resilient, charming, witty woman I've ever known, my mother, Janet.

My Mother and me at home in Huntington Woods, 1968

# Chapter 2: The Snowsuit Caper

*A fashionista is stylish even when no one else is looking…*
*oh bullshit! Everyone should know you're in town!*

Being one of nine children requires that you find a way to stand out in the crowd. And, little Janet, at six years old, was determined to make a splash on not just her family, but the world, starting with her rural community in Kentucky. Yup, from her neck of the "holler," she tried everything: "honky tonkin'" with her older sister (for city folk, that means late-night partying at the local hangout); standing on her desk in the middle of class yelling "Soooooweee!" to make a point; playing on the railroad tracks until dusk—forcing her mother to comb the hills with the neighbors to find her yelling at the top of her lungs; "Come in, you nighthawk!" And when she wasn't AWOL around home, in school Janet even had the bothersome habit of talking back to the principal, who also happened to be her brother-in-law, Charlie. (That's how things were in the South.) In fact, he delivered her first school paddling with the classic disclaimer, "This is going to hurt me more than it does you."

Janet's large family home rested on a grassy incline away from the road and the general store. It was surrounded by her mother's red, white, and pink rose garden for which she had won awards and even had a rose named after her (the "Belle B"). Fruit trees such as apple, peach, cherry, and even a few lovely magnolias adorned the green rolling landscape. Janet's favorite mulberry tree swayed like a luscious verdant fan on the right side of the house near the sun porch. She sat under it many days, feeling the thick soft grass, contemplating life, and later crying over her lost loves. It was also the practice location for Janet's cheerleading routines, the grass and soft earth providing a natural cushion for her famous flips and back bends. Farther up the hillside above the home place was a barn and a pen for hogs and chickens and an assortment of animals, including a brown and white cow named Daisy. The kids took care of the animals, until her parents became more prosperous and didn't need to rely on the livestock. The barn remained for a long time and provided a good playhouse for the kids.

Although the three-bedroom home wasn't able to hold all nine children at once, they were staggered in age so just the right number of kids was in the nest at any one time. But with such a large family, there was lots of hubbub on a daily basis.

They owned real estate all over the county and you could always see hired girls and workmen coming in and out of the house. But Daddy Warren made sure his children understood the value of money, often taking the kids to work to paint at their rental properties or to thin corn or pick berries at the farms of their sharecroppers. It all usually ended with a nice swim at Buckhorn, a camping site full of natural pools with crystal-clear water.

Belle and Warren had worked hard and saved their schoolteacher pay for many years to venture into business as the area's power couple, so to speak. Overall, their lifestyle was especially impressive compared to the small, cheaply constructed houses of families who lived on the "other side of the tracks." Unlike their neighbors, they had many modern conveniences (they were the only family for miles to have an indoor bathroom), including a two-car garage with an apartment above and the separate washhouse complete with a washing machine, a dryer, and a mangle for sheets and pillowcases. With so many children, washday was a big deal.

Even as well-respected and well off as Janet's family was, the kids wore hand-me-downs—partly because it was a traditional thing to do in a big family, but also a result of the Great Depression that had plagued the country since 1929. Much like the recession that enveloped another generation in 2008, the tough economy had no regard for a family's wealth or status. Everyone was hit hard, especially in rural, blue-collar areas where folks learned to cherish family and squeeze every dollar until it squealed. Janet's family was really one of the luckier ones. They even distributed "dole" food in their grocery store and gave credit to the miners so they could survive—and made out, still wealthy, after the worst of it.

Un-phased by trivial things like government cheese or an impending world war, Janet marched on, charming, or at the very least "pranking" her way into everyone's hearts. However, it wasn't until the "Snowsuit Caper" that Janet really succeeded in her effort to get the mountain folk to take notice. That's when she established herself as the Floyd County fashion plate, what we refer to nowadays as a "fashionista."

The year was 1938, the same year Hitler invaded Poland because he couldn't get into art school. It was also the year little Janet launched her own style invasion. Her particular struggle, her *Mein Kampf,* if you will, was with a world that allowed, and in her community practically required, hand-me-downs instead of pretty new dresses and handbags. Like every generation forced to suffer the consequences of its predecessors, Janet couldn't understand why she didn't have new clothes to wear. How could people throw on "anything" and live with themselves? It registered as the ultimate sign to Janet, at even that young, that if you didn't go out looking like a million bucks, you had no self-respect. And looking good definitely turned heads, a concept she grasped very quickly.

One morning, when the temperature dropped to sixteen degrees and heavy snow covered the ground like a thick quilt, Janet's mother made her wear something she found to be not only hideous, but the one thing never guaranteed with fashion, something *practical.* It was a brown snowsuit her older sister, Rita, had worn the previous year. Janet marveled why anyone could suffer such torture. With Rita's head in a book, Janet reasoned she couldn't see the dire consequences. And now, with the suit being too small for her, it was little Janet's turn. (If only you didn't have to grow up so you could keep all your favorite outfits!) The color of this monstrosity can only be described as puke-brown.

The consistency, well, let's say it was made of shiny-in-spots fabric that cried "poor" from every snag and puffy wrinkle. This was certainly not Janet's idea of making a fashion statement. It looked like her "splash" was indeed in serious peril.

As soon as her mother zipped up the suit, Janet headed out the door into the ever-present rolling landscape of white piled snow and slippery ice patches. She made her way down the long driveway to the narrow, curving, slick road. Then she navigated across the swinging bridge to the home of her best friend, Frannie, whose front porch was conveniently a mere fifteen steps from the bridge. Frannie lived in an area called Smacky Bottom, a little village full of colorful characters and local mischief, just as the name would suggest.

"Get in here, Janet!" cried Frannie from the pine wood porch that her father or grandfather had surely built by hand. Frannie had been peering out the front window and pushed open the screen door when she saw her friend navigating her way across the swaying bridge. Shaking off the sharp cold gust of air, Frannie rubbed her cold, rough hands together and blew on her small fingers until Janet trudged up the steps and they both scurried into the house.

Frannie was a thin girl with short red hair and green eyes. Like most folks in the area, she and Janet had known each other for as long as they could remember and they were instant friends. Frannie idolized Janet and saw her as a bright light illuminating the possibilities of a world beyond their sleepy holler. The two girls frequented the local theater to watch the movie stars in all their glamour, get updates on the news of the world, and escape the harsh realities of friends and neighbors stricken with polio, tuberculosis, and other conditions like black lung and pneumonia that ravaged hard-working families in coal towns like theirs.

Janet scooted up right next to the old wood-burning stove that blazed on in the living room, the flames making dancing patterns on the rough-hewn floorboards. Frannie's mother was out back in the cookhouse cleaning up after breakfast while her father, always up and out before dawn, was working in the coalmines that tunneled under every blade of grass and fork.

Janet threw her brown snowsuit off and in mere minutes she had amassed a pile of clothes in the middle of the room—a gray wool sweater, rubber galoshes, a scarf, her mittens, a hat, and of course, the dreaded suit. She rearranged the few remaining pieces of clothing that she did like and once she was satisfied with her school attire, Janet then shoved the snowsuit toward Frannie. "Here, you can wear this."

Frannie eagerly slid the snowsuit on and hugged herself into its warmth, beaming like she saw the movies stars do when they won an award. "Thank you, thank you!" she exclaimed before she stopped herself. "What will you wear?"

"Hand me your father's coat over there." Frannie picked up the well-worn, beige wool jacket from the kitchen table and handed it to her friend.

Janet looked it over, carefully examining its fashion potential. The sleeves were edged with coal stains and it reeked of tobacco. "Aw, heck with it!" she said, and threw the coat on the woodpile.

"Come on, you'll freeze to death!" Frannie looked at her, wide-eyed.

"Not if we run! Bet I'm faster!" Before Frannie knew what was happening, Janet pulled Frannie by her brown hood and darted past her and out into the cold. Her Mary Jane black patent leather shoes dove in and out of the snow piles as she flew back over the rickety swinging bridge.

Frannie quickly followed, slogging through the snow in her newly acquired puffy brown snowsuit, carrying her father's old miner's cap just in case. Because her legs were shorter than Janet's, it took her a while to catch up. At that point she started to chase Janet, holding out the miner's cap she had grabbed from the hook by the door.

"Put this on right now, young lady!" Frannie yelled, imitating Janet's mother.

"Ugg...leeeee!" cried Janet, looking back and smiling at her friend while the wind whipped around them.

The girls laughed as they took turns chasing each other through the streets all the way to school. The path led them along the roadside past the coal shafts jutting into the sky and coal trains lined up on the tracks that led to the center of town. There sat the hubbub of Garrett: a post office, police station, and a few stores, their wooden porches and posts covered in slush. There was Campbell's Grocery Store (a Conley building, very profitable), Hornsby's Drug Store, Frances Dress Shop, the old Evan's Haberdashery, and Coburn Lumber. (Marcella Coburn was Janet's classmate nemesis, always after her crush and boyfriend, though he didn't know it, Billy Logan. Eventually she snagged him, playing the role of his bride in their first grade play wedding.) But for an occasional truck, the roads were eerily silent. The early morning commuters had already made their way to work and school, eager to arrive before the next deluge of treacherous weather.

Garrett Elementary School popped out from around the bend with its red brick walls and parking lot full of yellow school busses. Cut-out snowflakes, white ticks on the glass from snowball fights, and construction paper drawings dotted the building's windows. With a big huff, the girls finally reached the large red metal double doors to get inside. Janet looked down at her red fingers and realized she had run three miles in the freezing cold, wearing only a cotton dress, long cotton stockings, underwear, and her Mary Janes. Needless to say, just about everything she put on that morning was left in a pile on the floor back at Frannie's house, except the snowsuit, which was now on Frannie.

As frozen as she was, there was no denying that Janet looked cute as a button and to prove it, she even did a catwalk through the halls. Mrs. Simms, one of the stricter homeroom teachers, a prim and proper Baptist lady, peered over her glasses when the girls made their tardy entrance, giving the still-shivering fashion plate a look of reproach as our star searched for a seat in the packed classroom. But Janet hadn't noticed her stare; she was enjoying her moment. The cotton dress was her favorite, a pretty pink one decorated with little red apple appliqués. Everything matched perfectly: the pink bow and stockings —even her panties had a convenient pocket for hiding the penny candy she'd lifted from her parents' general store the day before. Once she was satisfied that everyone had gotten a look, with a whistle of approval she plopped down at a desk and smiled—as did the boys.

For the next several wintry days, Janet and Frannie repeated the shedding ritual with Janet changing clothes at Frannie's house before they scurried off to class. However, being a small town, sightings of the girls, one severely underdressed and the other wearing the unmistakable brown snowsuit, circulated throughout the county. Belle, Janet's mother, got wind of their exploits and made a dash to the principal's office clutching yet another hand-me-down snowsuit which had belonged to her brother, Holden.

One day, after Janet got home from school, her mother was there to greet her, with a switch in hand that she had cut from the huge 100-year-old birch tree in her front yard. The next day, as a direct consequence of her rebellious actions, Janet proudly wore something new under her hand-me-downs, her little bottom, red as a tomato. It was a difficult lesson for Janet, but her classmates had surmised her fate. However, they also came to admire her strong will, bravery and, of course, uncommon fashion sense.

As she sat at her small desk in class that week, forced to wear yet another over-garment that she found to be totally unacceptable, her classmates went out of their way to compliment her on the "new" snowsuit and its unique color, a shade of green somewhere between rotten apples and jade. At that moment, Janet knew she had made the exact impact she was hoping for. The "splash" had worked. She had shown her mother, and the kids and teachers of Garrett, that she was an individual capable of making her own decisions, especially when it came to fashion. A "fashionista" was born. She had earned the respect of her peers who admired her courage and likely saw in her the same thing Frannie saw, a window into a world beyond the snowy mountains.

For the rest of that school year, while she may have looked drab on the outside at times, little Janet always made sure she wore something pretty underneath the hand-me-downs. In her mind she was always beautifully dressed; it would just take a little while longer before the rest of the world realized it.

# Chapter 3: Go Tell It on the Mountain

*When in doubt, kick 'em in the nuts and run like hell!*

You're Fred Astaire and I'm Ginger Rogers," said Janet, throwing a pair of trousers to Billy Jean.

"I'm Betty Grable," protested Billy Jean, throwing the pants over to Frannie.

"I want to be her. I look just like her," said Frannie, striking a vamp pose on the green summer grass.

"Sorry, Frannie, but you'd be a better Fred. Damn it, I'm Betty Grable!" Being an entrepreneur like her mother, Janet had agreed to pay her friends a quarter an hour to play any part she deemed appropriate. They even took her medicine for her (fifty cents for Black Draught, the dreaded cough syrup). To these less fortune across-the-tracks kids, it was a great deal.

Billy Jean, Frannie, and Janet continued with dress rehearsal while in full wardrobe, running their lines on the grassy hillside behind the Conley General Store with props they recently picked up from the sale rack. Playtime was mostly spent re-enacting famous films like *King Kong*, *Gone With the Wind*, comedies and westerns, and role playing all of the stars of the late thirties: Lana Turner, Betty Grable, Ginger Rogers, Vivian Leigh, Carole Lombard, Shirley Temple, Jean Harlow, Greta Garbo and Marlena Dietrich. Out of all the glamorous gals, Lana Turner was her favorite.

No genre was too tough for this trio of female thespians. They were eager to take on romantic roles, westerns, even fighting crime as The Green Hornet, or swinging on the laundry line as Sheena.

16

"I'm Sheena, Queen of the Jungle!" Janet roared from the top of the hill, in her Sheena outfit that consisted of a leopard scarf and leaves. "AHHHHH…AH …AHHHHH! Catch me!"

"Ok!" Billy Jean looked up at Janet precariously situating herself for adventure, and then went back to playing with her props, trying to un-crumple the netting over her blue pillbox hat.

Wearing long silk gloves, Janet grabbed the laundry line and slid down with a *whoooooosh!* Off she'd sail—usually into a strawberry patch at the end of the lawn just by the road, leaving her friends far behind. Her heroics meant many scuffed knees, but for her it was so worth it!

By studying her favorite actors, Janet became quite the artist, drawing outfits and storyboarding adventures from dog-eared comic books or smudged newspaper funnies. Next she moved on to sketching and creating outfits, which would later on be the dresses she'd have custom-made in Cincinnati and Detroit as a model.

On rainy days, in contrast to her outdoor shenanigans, she really loved to play with paper dolls. When Janet was growing up, it was a popular pastime. Girls would order magazines and cut out dolls that were based on fashion models and popular stars. Janet's favorite paper doll was of Lana Turner and she bought her tons of designer clothes. Every paper outfit money could buy was on and off that doll—from summer casual to high couture. Janet began learning the language of style from a young age. Her friends, however, didn't share her fascination, so she usually ended up playing with her sister, Rita. Janet and Rita would have contests to determine who could dress her doll more glamorously. Once the winner was crowned, they'd celebrate with a tea party. "We loved it especially on rainy days when we would set up our dream homes on the second floor of the store, the rain hitting the roof of the building, and it felt so wonderful." They'd use the store's blankets to represent the important places in town, the pink blankets for the restaurant, blue blankets for home, and white blankets for the celebratory gala tea party. It was quite the spread, and the girls were enamored with their resourcefulness and their stunning competitors.

As often happens, Rita was the polar opposite of her younger sister. She didn't socialize with the kids across the tracks or go out of her way to talk to many people. She was tall and elegant, a combination many of her peers labeled as "stuck up," claiming that she must be too good for the "riff raff." She reminded Janet of the main character from *Alice in Wonderland* with her headband, simple A-line yellow flowered dress, and classy tailored look she usually wore. Soon, it all fell into place when Rita played the lead in *Alice in Wonderland*. Naturally Janet was jealous, but she was just a little squirt at six years old. They needed an older woman. Rita was eight.

When she wasn't playing dolls, Rita was practicing the piano. Just two years older than Janet, Rita had her heart set on being a concert pianist which fit nicely with her sister's dreams of being on the silver screen.

After Janet would return from spending her afternoon staring wide-eyed at the latest movie, she would coax Rita to accompany her on the piano while she performed a song in front of a full-length mirror in the Conley living room. In that moment she would inhabit the character, imitating the latest song and dance routine: Betty Grable, Carmen Miranda, Shirley Temple…they all eventually appeared in the Conley living room as channeled through a very determined six-year-old.

When Janet didn't have her friends or brothers and sisters to play movies or dolls with, she was quite content to entertain herself. Her day would start when her mom cooked pork chops, eggs, fried apples, and biscuits in the dawn light before she left for the day. Both parents minded the grocery store or collected rent from the many properties they owned around town. After eating breakfast, Janet was unsupervised for the most part, even at six years old; she was out the door either to school or if it was a vacation day or the weekend, she was on her own. Typically, the parents left the older children in charge. Now it was Anne who supervised her siblings, that is until she married and left the nest. That left only five of out nine total children living at home. After college, Edward and Mitchell joined the service and once Anne left, the others, Rita, Laura, Holden, Janet, Duke, and little Beth took full advantage by running roughshod throughout the countryside. Okay, well, mainly Janet ran roughshod throughout the countryside.

Like most small-town children who are bored and unsupervised, Janet wasted no time creating her share of mischief—pushing over outhouses on Halloween, playing on the railroad tracks, occasionally hopping on empty train cars to get around—anything to pass the time while waiting to be called for dinner. Since her parents owned the store, Janet assumed that it was just like at home, things were hers for the taking. And because she had always been taught to be considerate of others, Janet would ask folks what they needed and she'd nonchalantly fill her shopping list and make deliveries on her way home. Her philanthropy extended beyond her own social circle and she'd often visit elderly neighbors and lift their spirits with a treat from the shop and sometimes an impromptu song from the *Good Ship Lollypop* or *Yankee Doodle Dandy*.

When her parents worked in the evening, usually Janet would cross the dirt road, over the train tracks and the swinging bridge to visit Frannie and all her friends in Smacky Bottom. During her journey one day, she met a neighbor she rarely saw. He lived in one of their four rental houses up on the hill behind Conley General Store. Anne lived in one of these houses after she married Charlie Clark, a protégé of Alice Crocker Lloyd, a prominent educator and, of course, the elementary school principal. She was anxious to show Anne and Charlie her new outfit—just in time to get some chicken and dumplings. By then her little bottom was over the (many) school disciplinary actions and her spirits were as high as ever.

"Janet," Mr. Ballad called out, "Come see my new chickens."

"Ok. Any little ones?" Janet turned abruptly and headed towards his chicken coop on the side of his front porch. She was curious; she wanted to see the fake egg farmers often put under a chicken to coax it to lay a real egg.

"There are new chicks," said the neighbor, showing Janet into the henhouse. "I'll set you up on this shelf and I'll gather a few eggs and show you how I do it." Janet walked into the chicken house, her nose overwhelmed by the pungent, stale odor. She wore a new white poplin dress her mother had just bought her with a blue silk ribbon belt and a matching blue ribbon in her dark blonde hair. Painfully aware of the risk of getting her new dress dirty, she stepped ever so carefully into the weathered structure.

"Ok." She looked around, ready to observe.

Mr. Ballard lifted Janet on the ledge, her little dress spread out on the shelf, then in one movement, he put his hand up her leg and she, with a shock, felt his fat fingers go under her panties and touching the rim of her private parts. Terrified, she screamed louder than hell.

"Ahhhhhhh! Ballard, you old son of a bitch!" She kicked him in the stomach, pushed him away with her little Mary Jane shoes, and jumped down from ledge, still screaming as she ran down the hill.

"I'm going to tell my Daddy on you! He'll put you in the 'tinury!' " She ran as fast as she could back home.

Often when it was nighttime and she was all alone, she would think about what had happened to her in that chicken coop: an experience that would affect her deeply and cast a shadow throughout her life. Events like that made the hours she spent at the movie theater even more important. It was a place where she felt safe, where she could dream about a life beyond the dusty dirt roads, a life free of people like Mr. Ballard, a life where you were *somebody*. As she watched beautiful ladies and dashing men sing and dance on the flickering screen in front of her, she was sure they never had to face such horrible things. They looked so happy and carefree that she was certain they never cried silently in a dark movie theater.

We all have struggles and obstacles to overcome, and Janet certainly had her share as she grew up in the close-knit rural community seemingly cut off from the rest of the world by imposing mountains and punishing winters. And it is an unfortunate reality that cruelty and intimidation often bubbled just under the surface, rarely talked about in a culture layered with neighborly courtesy, good manners, and even religious overtones. To make matters worse, children were taught not to talk back and not to question the adults in the community. They were to do as they were told, because grownups always knew best.

However, even at the tender age of six, Janet was strong-willed and had a reputation for questioning authority, not rudely of course, but she was not shy about expressing her feelings. Had she not been of such a mind, she may not have escaped the lecherous Mr. Ballard and his creepy chicken coop. She never did tell anyone about the incident, especially her father (until she confided in me). Sticking up for yourself was one thing, but accusing an adult of such an act, especially since it was sexual in nature, was just not done. And Janet knew that.

Naturally things have changed a great deal in that small community over the following decades and just like the rest of the world, information has empowered children to better realize when something is wrong and be able to get the help they need. However, Janet always used this incident as a reminder that no matter how idyllic and nostalgic a childhood may be, it's never perfect—unless, somehow she could will it so. And, if someday, she had a child, nothing of that magnitude would happen to her son or daughter. Her child would always be safe. Always.

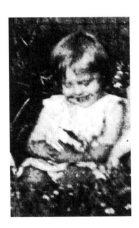

Little Janet

# Chapter 4: Mammoth Cave

*When the going gets tough, the tough get Gucci!*

When I was in school, I was on a search for my own identity. As is typical, I was determined to be just like my mother while in elementary school and then nothing like her as I moved on to higher grades. However, there was no denying my DNA and being Janet's daughter, I participated mostly in the arts, printmaking, painting, drawing, chorus, and of course securing the lead in high school plays. And, I too learned early that in the limelight was a magical place to stand.

Anytime I'd share an event of the day in the hope for approval (like when I got the lead in the spring show), Janet would invariably wax poetic on her days as the "best cheerleader this side of the Daniel Boone Mountain Parkway." And maybe she was. I don't really know for certain, but what I do know is that she never failed to regale me with stories of her triumphs. Throughout my life as she would tell me these sometimes fantastical tales, I was never certain how to extrapolate true events from "Southern spin."

However, there was no denying that my mother made the most of her early foray into the limelight as a star cheerleader. It was a place she felt incredibly comfortable and she was certain this would somehow help her move on to bigger and better things. In the spring of 1946 she tried out as an incoming freshman at Garrett High and was unanimously chosen as the youngest squad captain ever. Janet's only real competitor had been Rebecca Martin whose family later established a well-known chain of department stores in Chicago and throughout the country. Rebecca and Janet were always neck and neck for everything: being star of the school play, attracting the cutest boy in class, scoring the best seat in assembly.

Being similarly talented and equally driven, it was an adversarial relationship at best. Each publically wished the other well while secretly longing for a talent that the other lacked. Rebecca was named valedictorian that year while Janet won the 4-H star camper award that summer and in the fall was elected freshman class president. It went on and on and back and forth, as if they were the only two young girls in town.

Although brainy, Rebecca clearly had her challenges. She didn't have the outgoing personality Janet did. For the life of her, she could not throw a great party, dance any of the popular dances, balance notebooks and pencils on her stomach while doing a back bend, kiss boys, or shoot a gun from a moving truck. Rebecca was also utterly useless in a cafeteria food fight. Worst of all, she couldn't do splits, a cardinal sin in Janet's eyes. I also surmised from her stories that while my mother was often the life of the party (even when there was technically no party), Rebecca was the exact opposite. She was one of those girls that was so mannered the other school kids found her to be a prude. There was even a joke going around that if she ever had children they would have to be conceived by Immaculate Conception or delivered by stork. Notoriously snobby, Rebecca had started rumors, with great pride, that she was going to Bryn Mawr, an elite yet obscure college in the East. Her compatriots nodded their head in approval while likely being totally clueless. Besides, what on earth was a Bryn Mawr? Most of the locals thought it some kind of fishing lure.

At the end of that freshman year, all of the current cheerleaders were asked to do a cheer at assembly for the entire crowd so they could vote on next year's captain. Janet declined since she was busy beating up a couple of younger boys who had been pestering her little sister that day. "They have seen me every night practically since I was six! Heck, they know what I've got," she reasoned. Janet had played the role of Garrett Falcon's basketball team mascot from first grade to seventh grade and had been middle school cheerleading captain. She had already exercised her dramatic muscles as the team's mascot, flipping her way into the hearts of all the boys. In fact, this is where she built the foundation for her future in cheerleading. She saw this as just the first step in a journey to bigger things. She was so intent on building her dream that she threw herself wholeheartedly into the task, cheering and encouraging the team through each game. Her unmistakable booming voice during cheers became her calling card, so much so that she chose to leave the megaphone perched nearby, showing that she didn't need the help. The game announcers in the press booth were so impressed they nicknamed her "Mammoth Cave." In fact, the nickname stuck with her through college.

She was sure that she would just walk into high school sophomore year with the coveted role of captain based on her star status and her freshman performance alone. She couldn't have been more wrong.

Janet had not only rested on her laurels, but she had underestimated the power of the snooty Rebecca and her "Becca-ites," the catty lackeys that followed her like a pigtailed wave of approval wherever she went. Rebecca and her sensibly coifed gang had done quite a bit of campaigning against my mother. Not only that, she had apparently been practicing a lot because she managed to master a running flip into a split (not completely to the ground). It was not really well executed, but it was just enough to turn the tide against the fashion-conscious and feisty Janet, who wasn't willing to jump on command that fateful day.

With ten days to go to before graduation, over 400 kids crowded into the school auditorium to see who was posted as cheerleading captain for 1947 . For the most part, Garrett High kids only cared about who was going to the prom with whom, who dated Tyler Hall the captain of the football team, and who would be the captain of the cheerleaders—their new queen, popularity trendsetter, and spiritual leader.

Janet pranced, with a huge black bow bouncing in her Garbo-type hairdo, over to the sheet of paper where a crowd of teens pressed in to see the carefully typed list. Out of the corner of her eye, she saw Rebecca jump in the air and yell out a triumphant scream that rivaled any 'Mammoth Cave' shout, "YIPPPPPEEEEEEEEEEE!!!!"

It was one that echoed all the way through the mountains to Lexington and pierced Janet's heart. Still not willing to concede, Janet pushed her way through the gathering of teens and stared at the piece of paper on the wall. There, in black and white, were the most painful words Janet could imagine: *Captain − Rebecca Martin.*

Not only had Janet Lee not made captain, she was not even on the cheerleading team! Janet gripped her chest while Rebecca looked on, laughing wickedly. The crowd "ooooed" and "ahhhhhed" with mixed emotion, waiting to see how my mother would react to the news. Classmates can be a cruel bunch, willing to change allegiances at the drop of a hat or the crowning of a title. Janet had a small bit of satisfaction when she saw Janie May Morris, her playmate since kindergarten and not so popular size 18 friend, start to slug Rebecca. The Becca-ites quickly circled around their wicked queen like a Salem coven circling the devil's pentacle on the ground.

"I'll get you, Rebecca Martin, just you wait," Janet said after she had shaken off the shock and regained her composure.

"I'm waiting…" Rebecca stuck her nose in the air, "…to start practice with my new team. Go Black Devils!" After a lame leap in the air and a few chuckles from the crowd, she sped off in her white saddle bucks, entourage in tow.

Devastated but not defeated, Janet Lee vowed never to lose her place in a competition again, never to rest on her laurels, and never to take anything for granted. Maybe this was just the kick in the ass she needed. The star athlete and now former cheerleader was still the daughter of one of the powerful families in the county, and she would not go down without a fight. After all, she was Warren and Belle Conley's daughter.

Janet had learned a thing or two from that experience—humility and defeat—and her junior year would tell a very different story. Understanding the power of hard work and humility, Janet made plans to take back the cheerleading crown. Every chance she got, she practiced handsprings into a standing flip and splits on the grassy hill in front of her parents, the preacher, and anyone else who congregated at the general store.

"Dad! Watch me!" Janet called out to her father. She ran as fast as she could, did a cartwheel to a flip, landing on her feet with her hands in the air. "Go Black Devils!" she turned back, out of breath, to see that her father had disappeared. A group of men stood on the porch staring at the young girl with her arms outstretched, feeling slightly silly.

"You go, Janet!" cried one of the miners.

It was an all-too-familiar scene for Janet and her siblings. As a successful business owner, with the store and many rental properties, the customers always came first, leaving the kids to encourage and in some sense, parent themselves—an unfortunate tradeoff for the wealth the family enjoyed.

On a very crisp and unusually cool Friday night in September, excitement filled the air. The big event was on: the dual between Janet Lee and Rebecca for title of Cheerleading Team Captain. The Garrett High student body had been anticipating the showdown for months.

On that day, the entire county was there, even the rival school over in or "up" Wayland (as they say in the local vernacular), another town mostly filled with mining folks. People staked out their territory on the cold metal bleachers waiting for the show. It was common knowledge that these archrivals were in it for blood and in a matter of moments they would know who ruled the roost. As dusk crept over the mountains, the stadium lights snapped on, ensuring that the audience could clearly see the bright green turf below. The Falcon's scoreboard sign blinked excitedly: "Rebecca" and "Janet Lee" spelled out in lights against the blue mountain horizon.

Rebecca went first. Wearing that damn bow of hers and a fitted white turtleneck, she waved to her dedicated minions. She let out a rebel yell, ran into two handsprings, a backflip, and then a split all the way to the ground. The crowd cheered. It was seriously the best she had ever done. Janet was stunned. How could she beat that?

Slowly but confidently, Janet stepped onto the field as she tried to hide her shaking hands. She wore her favorite black-and-orange cheer skirt, matching black shirt, and her hair in a high tight ponytail with an orange ribbon. As a secret surprise, her panties read in black lettering, "GO BLACK DEVILS !"

The crowd erupted with enthusiasm when the well-liked teen walked onto the field, taking her place. Janet took a deep breath and started to run as fast as her legs would move her. She sprang into backflips all the way down the fifty yard line, let loose her best "Mammoth Cave" rebel yell, then ran back down the center line springing into front flips around the stadium to "ooooo's" and "ahhhhh's." It was a combination that no one had done before and the spectators jumped out of their seats, cheering the determined girl on. Energized by their reaction, she then did a row of standing flips, a one-handed cartwheel, and a no-handed cartwheel rounding up to the big finish: running down to the goal posts, her white Keds gleaming. This was the finale she had been feverishly rehearsing for months: a handspring, then a double flip into a split. Yes! "Go Garrett!" she yelled, her pom-poms raised triumphantly in the air, shimmering in the tungsten glare.

She held the pose as she had always been taught, waiting for a response from the crowd, hoping it had looked as great as it felt. At first it was almost silent, the crowd stood with mouths agape for a split second before they broke into a huge roar like she had never heard. They went wild. Rebecca literally fainted, her Becca-ites quickly rushing to revive her.

Once the crowd simmered down, Janet stood in the spotlight, panting and ecstatic, sweat pouring over her well-made-up little face and ruby red lips. All of her hard work had paid off. She had felt the sting of defeat and didn't like it one bit. She searched the faces in the stands to find her father, but he wasn't there. However, she didn't have time to worry about that. Janet was back with a vengeance. The crowd was roaring yet again, celebrating their new cheerleading captain, relishing a return to the way things used to be with Janet leading the team to one victory after another. She received a fifteen minute standing ovation, something that had never happened in the history of the small town. The applause and bright lights held her in a trance. She beamed. There was nothing like it. Nothing.

Janet was back in the center of the student body, in her rightful place: and no one would ever take that away from her again.

From Janet's high school year book 1946

# Chapter 5: Four Roses

*There's nothing more handsome than a man with ambition.*

As she grew up and began to mature, experiencing victory and defeat in high school, Janet had already tasted the bitterness of life's lessons. She found, for instance, that the chicken coop incident wasn't an isolated one. Being a female and an attractive one at that—during that era especially—posed many challenges for such a strong-willed woman. She quickly learned that it was a man's world and being female, she would have to figure out how to navigate it as best she could. Despite her valiant efforts, she still faced harassment and unwanted advances from bosses, politicians, and other "upstanding" citizens in the community that included friends, husbands, fathers, and even brothers. In one incident, she was even groped by a "good Samaritan" while helping her up from a fall at school. She had decided to approach men with caution, always, until they had earned her trust while ironically wanting their adoration all the while: in essence, what we call a "Southern tease."

Another of life's hard truths was facing death, and she did so as a young girl of eight. It began with the untimely passing of her brother Holden, at age seventeen. His car lost control and slid off the steep mountain road during a weekend visit from Summer College. Janet admired her brother immensely and they shared a strong bond. In him, she saw a handsome Southern gentleman just starting to make his way in the world, and she planned to follow in his footsteps as soon as she was able. He had the same charisma and charm Janet did, and was arguably the best-looking of all the boys. However, as often happens among siblings, they had their disagreements. There was a heated quarrel on the night before his accident. She didn't recall why. As he was leaving to see his girlfriend, she screamed at him for the whole house to hear. "I hope you die tomorrow!" And he did.

Despite the challenges faced growing up in the tough mountain town, Janet was nothing if not resilient. As she moved through adolescence and grew into a young woman, she began to appreciate the attention she had always gotten from the opposite sex. She would learn a lot about love and loss, as she navigated the limited local dating pool.

Her first real romantic infatuation was at the young age of twelve. During a high school after-basketball-game party she met a dashing young man who had ambitious plans of serving his country. Danny was four years older than Janet, but she had always been mature for her age. They got away from the crowd and sat in his car listening to music and talking. At that first meeting, he told Janet how much he loved her and when she was old enough he would like to marry her. Indeed, two weeks later, he introduced Janet to his family. "They are such wonderful, high-class people," Janet thought, and their wealth was obvious, as was her desire to associate with the crème de la crème of society.

Soon Danny was back at the Virginia Military Academy and that left Janet to wrestle with her fervent imagination. When she sat all alone in the dark theater looking up wide-eyed at the latest movie, she imagined herself and Danny in the lead roles: she would be preparing for a wedding, waiting for him to return from overseas service, and eventually living in a beautiful mansion, somewhere in the South, naturally, planning a family of polite, well-groomed children. Janet even modeled my childhood room to be exactly like Danny's beautiful sister Alicia's room: red cherry wallpaper, antebellum Miss Scarlett Madame Alexander dolls on the shelves, and a huge billowy canopy bed complete with *Gone with the Wind* ruffles and pageantry.

But her dreams were dashed when she saw a group of her girlfriends slowly approaching her front porch with dour expressions one Saturday afternoon. Upon learning that Danny and three of his buddies had been killed in a tragic car accident, she was devastated. To make matters worse, her mother wouldn't allow her to attend the funeral in Chase, Virginia. She was protective of her young daughter, but, being so young, Janet saw it as yet another unfairness in her small and increasingly harsh world.

Three years later, Janet met an intriguing young man while walking with two of her girlfriends to town on their way to the movies. He was gorgeous, a tall Warren Beatty lookalike with brown hair and blue eyes. He was well-dressed with a gorgeous physique, and driving a powder blue convertible with red leather interior. All the girls went crazy over him (and probably a few of the guys, too, if we're being honest).

The handsome young man asked the group if they wanted a ride. They immediately agreed, that is, except for Janet.

"I don't even know you," she reasoned.

"You don't know me? Hi, I'm David Hall," he laughed. He seemed intrigued by her refusal, which was apparently something that he was not accustomed to.

"Well, I'm Janet Lee Conley, do you know me?" she retorted. The doe-eyed girls finally talked her into getting in his car.

"Ok, but I'm not sitting in the back," she warned.

So she sat in front with David and they were on their way to much more than just a leisurely drive down the road. They fell headfirst into that young, all-consuming love we tend to experience as young adults. Eventually, as she had with Danny, they talked about marriage: life on the top of a hill with a big house and maybe even a helicopter to take them to Lexington to shop or go to school. Janet soon met the entire family and they were sweet and wonderful, but like many in the hardscrabble area, they were riddled with unspeakable tragedy. His two sisters died of TB (tuberculosis) and even his brother Paul would meet an untimely death.

However, there was no denying the chemistry between the two and when they would visit their respective hometowns it was like they were like royalty—a beautiful distraction for the small communities. David worked with his father on their oil wells ("just like the movie

*Giant*," Janet romanced) and had a promising future. They were definitely the talk of the towns.

But as with most fairy tales, underneath there was a darker side. Janet began to notice that David could be quite possessive and to make matters worse, he had a penchant for speeding off in his car and had already been in a few bad accidents. With fast cars becoming increasingly common, the small country roads were no match for the revved up engines combined with the surging hormones of teenage boys. It could be a deadly combination, and Janet was already sensitive to the danger after her brother's death.

One summer day, they picked up a friend of David's to go swimming. The friend lit Janet's cigarette and she gave him a peck on the cheek to thank him for being "such a gentleman." Janet was a flirt and liked to keep her men on their toes. David was furious. He shunned her at the swimming hole, and when they got back in car the other guy was obviously not invited to return home. Giving her the silent treatment for the entire ride, he finally stopped in front of her family's store and said, "I'm going to Heinemann." That was a "wet county" where she knew he could buy liquor. So many kids were killed because they had to drive over long mountain roads to buy alcohol.

"David," Janet sensed this was wrong. "Stay with me!" She insisted a few more times until he pulled away. They were supposed to go out dancing later. Janet however felt the uncomfortable ride home surely meant he'd speed again on the country roads, to parts unknown. Her stomach had that knot we often get before bad news.

"You can't go, honey girl," said David. "So long, honey girl. Send me four roses!" He screeched off so fast gravel flew all over the place, leaving Janet in a cloud of dust and confusion.

That evening she wore a new yellow cotton sundress, strapless, trimmed with a little white ruffle across the top of the neckline and finished it off with white sandals. She positioned herself, lying across the daybed on the sun porch so she could see David when he pulled up the driveway. Time passed. He should have been there ten minutes ago. While looking in her compact and checking her lipstick, she heard her cousin Aline calling out from the gate.

"Janet! Janet, David's been killed," she screamed.

Janet couldn't believe her. "That's impossible."

Aline opened the gate, "Janet, David's had a wreck and he's dead! It's true!"

Janet dropped her compact, her makeup purse spilling its contents all over the concrete, and ran to her daddy inside their store. "Daddy, David's been killed! Aline said David had a wreck. Take me. Take me to the hospital!"

Her father didn't say a word. He got his keys and walked quietly to his pickup truck with Janet hurrying behind him. Once inside, the wind was blowing her hair from the open window as she sat in the passenger seat, like the many times she sat next to David in his convertible. As she stared out the window, things seemed to be moving in slow motion. The accident site was on the route to the hospital. It started to register when she rounded the dangerous mountainous curve and saw a crowd gathered around David's crushed convertible. "Oh God, Daddy, there's his car, there he is!" She jumped out of the truck and ran across the road to the car. David had already been taken to the hospital. The car was in a ditch, jutting out from under a cliff. People milled around, murmuring and shaking their heads while the radiator hissed its last remaining breath.

As she studied the scene in disbelief, Janet saw tiny pieces of paper strewn around the car, apparently spilling out from the dash compartment. She couldn't make out the contents of the note, but she recognized her own handwriting on the pieces. Whatever the message had been, it looked as if David had hastily shredded it, taking its contents with him into eternity. The police indicated that the car must have been traveling over 100 miles per hour and veered off the road through a cornfield and back on the road before losing control and careening into the mountainside. The impact was great enough to cause a loose bolder to fall on him, breaking his neck—a freak occurrence. Without that final impact, he may have lived and Janet's life would have likely turned out much different—not better or worse, just different. To this day, Janet doesn't remember writing David that letter strewn on his dash. Or what could have possibly triggered his suicide other than extreme jealousy that day at the lake. As soon as David told Janet he was off to get whiskey, she knew it would not end well. She remembers pleading with him to stay, and failing—a fatal mistake that has stayed with her and changed her outlook on life.

Janet walked, almost in a trance, back across the road to her father. "Daddy, take me to the hospital. They say he's there." And so her father turned the pickup around and they drove to the hospital only about three minutes away. Her dad had remained silent the entire time. He knew exactly what she felt and what she wanted to do. The kids had always been somewhat afraid of her daddy. It was a time when men were supposed to remain stoic and imposing, ruling their family with an iron hand. But he wasn't always that way. With his first child, Anne, he was present for her. She was daddy's girl and they shared a strong bond. Janet had heard the stories of how he read to Anne every night, kissing her sweetly as she fell asleep. It was a relationship she envied.

Near the entrance of Lackey Hospital, Janet saw people outside sitting on a fence.

"There's no use in going in now," one man yelled. "He's dead, Janet."

*Bastard*, she thought. Of course she paid him no mind and walked in through the double doors while her father waited patiently outside. In her heart, she still denied the reality unfolding before her. She hurried down the long hallway and pushed her way through the gawkers and hospital staff until she reached the doorframe of the cold, clinical room.

David was lying on a gurney, full length, stretched out. He didn't have a scratch on him. His hair wasn't even mussed. His clothes neat as always. He had a sailor hat beside him that Janet had given him, the one he loved to wear.

*He's so beautiful*, Janet thought. David, looked as perfect as ever, almost sleeping. "He's not dead. He's not dead. He can't be," she protested.

His mother, Ann, looked up from weeping over her son and asked Janet, "I know you two were together today. What were his last words to you?"

Through her tears, Janet responded. "Ann, he said 'Send me four roses.'"

Janet kissed him on the forehead, knowing this was the last time she'd ever see him. Then she was walking down the hospital hallway and out the door, all the while in shock not believing what she just saw: that she could actually leave him there. A part of her felt she would see him later for her date. What was a normal, hopeful day had gone in a direction so horribly wrong that she couldn't get her mind around it. It was almost like a helpless betrayal—how could she be alive and he not there anymore?

Without a word, her daddy opened the pickup door, Janet climbed in, and they headed home. A few minutes later, Janet saw Paul, David's brother, and his buddy Jimmy at the gas station. She asked her dad to pull over. She wanted to be with her friends. Janet jumped out. She gave him a quick hug. "Bye, Daddy, thank you." He felt her sorrow, and she knew it. That ride with her father during the tragedy of David's death was the closest she ever felt to him. (Unfortunately, when she was twenty-one, Janet lost her father to a drowning accident.)

Janet and Paul spent that evening together, crying, talking, making funeral arrangements, and coordinating with the family and the funeral director. A wreath of white roses was ordered, with four red roses in the center. They bonded after David's death like a brother and sister. She felt closer to David when she was with Paul, only to have him, too, die in a car accident a year later.

The next day, the funeral was held at the Hall's large house, which in those days was common. The Hall residence was very much like the Conley home in stature, a quick county away, a gorgeous plantation-style house, with large white porch pillars holding vigil for the lost promise of a sweet young man.

After the service, Ann approached Janet when she saw her wreath of white roses interlaid with four red roses on the stand near his coffin. "At the hospital when you told me what he said, did you mean seventy-four roses, dear? That's what the florist sent over."

Janet realized there was some confusion. Ann had laid a wreath of seventy-four roses on his coffin. "Well, Ann, I think he did say that. So you're right, seventy-four roses." She didn't have the heart to tell Ann that David, when he mentioned four roses, was talking about a brand of alcohol.

Along with the misinterpreted variations on a theme of flower arrangements to add to her misery, before they closed the casket, Janet allowed the funeral director to put a picture of her in David's hands. While it felt right at the time, that image, and regrets about lying to David's mother, has haunted her throughout her adult life. Amidst the pain, however, she does, true to form, remember her outfit. In her teen years, her mother saw her flair for fashion and started buying and making clothes for her to wear. She was definitely dressed to pay tribute to her beautiful David, lying like a prince in state, amidst the hill folk paparazzi.

Janet wore a white dress, lavender sandals and a silk sash, lavender hanky and pearls, her hair in a soft wave with a lavender hat and netting—her makeup, of course, beautiful, as if more dates with David were in store. Only later, after the shock of her father's death, did she realize she wore the exact same outfit to David's funeral that Holden's girlfriend, Audrey, wore to Holden's funeral.

In September, on Janet's sixteenth birthday, she enrolled early admittance into the University of Kentucky and signed up for a full class load of twenty-six credits. For her living situation, Belle bought a house in Lexington for Janet and Rita on Leader Avenue. Actually, she bought two houses—one across the street to watch over her girls. In those days, girls had to be chaperoned if they did not live in the dorm.

After two months, Rita left the university to do her student teaching so Janet was left to her own devices. Her days and nights were consumed by wild parties with the football team, bar hopping, and drinking rather than studying or attending classes. While Janet's mother was looking for a chaperone/roommate for her, Janet found Marylyn Jennings or "Mert" and her good-looking brother, Paul, who reportedly gave Janet her first French kiss—which, by the way, she didn't enjoy to the tune of a slap across the face. Like many freshmen that fall, the two co-eds searched for the hottest party spots in town.

That's when they found the Jolly Trolley where Janet first heard about Bill, the man who would eventually be my father. So, there was a light at the end of the tunnel, although Janet didn't know it yet. Sadly, the impact of David's death, combined with the stress of college, was all too much. She dropped half of her credits and still missed classes, drank daily, and cried at night clutching David's picture.

Her mother sensed her change in behavior. One afternoon she made an unexpected visit to the house on Leader Avenue. Before knocking, she somehow knew to walk behind the house, only to find liquor bottles piled high against the back. Belle acted immediately. This time it wasn't a birch branch; it was the thoughtful love of a worried parent who guided her back home to complete her freshman year.

Janet enrolled in the local Pikeville College, a great little institution tucked safely away only two hours from Garrett. That's where she continued as a cheerleader, lived in a dormitory, and learned to put David's tragedy behind her. Her grades were good, her cheerleading even better, so much so that the president of the college asked her to teach the cheers to the student body. Janet threw herself into college life and even ran the assemblies before classes.

First there was the Morning Prayer and then Janet would get up on stage and lead the audience in the new cheers by acting them out. She learned how to break down the cheers and have the students repeat them back to her. In no time, they were chanting the catchy phrases she had carefully rehearsed in her dorm room. She discovered that she had natural charisma and a flair for performing onstage: and that talent became her lifeline, always thinking the spotlight was on her— whether under the lights with the smell of greasepaint, or not.

Janet as a teen sunning at the local lake in Kentucky

# Chapter 6: The Jolly Trolley

*Go where the fashion takes you, and never look back!*

The lights of the Jolly Trolley, a lively little trolley car turned drinking establishment in Lexington, Kentucky, off the UK campus, shone brightly as Marilyn or "Mert" and Janet stepped out of the yellow cab in their finest evening garb and swished their way to the welcoming pub. Janet had on a beautiful yellow sundress, backless, with high-heeled black sandals and Mert, the well-built brunette from Lexington, a red skirt and white chiffon blouse. The new roomies tootled around the town drinking and flirting with guys 24-7. They were on a roll—with a three-date-a-day minimum for breakfast, lunch, and dinner.

The girls looked fabulous! They were following the mantra my mother has repeated to me more times than I can count: "You never know when a young beau might sweep you off your feet!" At sixteen, Janet was doing her best to see all the world has to offer. She had to start somewhere, so The Jolly Trolley it was.

"Hello girls!" Owner Tommy McGill was popular with most underclassmen at the university, the wide-eyed kids naturally being some of his best customers. "What can I get for you ladies, a milkshake?" he said as he habitually whipped out a rag and wiped the counter down.

"Yes, with lots of whipped cream on top," answered Mert. In no time, he was back with a colorful frozen treat.

"Really, Tommy? What's this?" asked Janet.

"A Pink Lady," answered Tommy.

"Any alcohol in this stuff?" Mert questioned.

"Loaded!" he smiled. It was a regular milkshake, which the girls believed was full of spirits. They wasted no time in slurping it down, brain freezes be damned! (Even though the drinking age was 21, the girls attempted to charm bartenders into looking the other way. Most of the time they got alcohol from frat boys or upper classmen.)

Unfortunately, tonight the atmosphere was no match for their optimism. "This place is dead, Tommy! We dressed up and everything! Where is everyone?" asked Janet.

"Oh, on campus the Sigma Nu's are having a football and beer chugging contest. If I know your classmates, half of the school will be there," he responded as he began filling pints.

"How droll! Such hicks and farm boys. It's a miracle any man grows up at all!" Janet smirked.

"Thank god we're GDIs..." Mert piped up.

"GDIs?" asked Tommy.

"God damn independents!" both girls chimed at once.

"Well, we're just going to have to find more mature men," Janet said, emphasizing her drawl as she tended to do when she was out on the town. She had learned as a young girl to turn up the Southern charm when looking for a man.

"Real men..." Mert slapped her hand down on the bar in a definitive gesture. Peanuts went flying.

"Well, now, I'm sure we got some real men around here somewhere..." Tommy gestured half-heartedly as he scooped up the peanuts.

The girls looked over at the gentlemen almost nodding off in a booth against the wall and then back at Tommy.

"Hell, Momma always taught me to make the best of a situation so I say you can't have a party without music." Janet slinked over to the jukebox and stared through the thick glass, studying each song title as the record flipped over.

She let out a yell. "Woo! I love 'Boogie Woogie Bugle Boy!'" No sooner had she squealed when the Andrews Sisters started blasting through the speakers, piercing the silence with the infectious harmonies. Janet and Mert jumped up and started doing The Jitter

Bug, waving over at the "group of grandpas" that were admiring them from afar.

"I bet you couldn't dance to it on the bar," challenged Tommy. "Free drinks all night!"

"Hell yeah!" Agile Janet kicked off her high heels and gracefully hopped on the bar and began shimmying along the narrow plank. She looked down at the shiny surface and could see her footprints as she made her way back and forth for all to see.

I can only imagine the sight of my mother, young and carefree, kicking her heels up on top of the bar as locals looked on. No doubt she was in her element, awash in the attention she was surely receiving. It was mere happenstance that her future was only minutes away.

Mert looked out the picture window and spotted Pinky and his sidekick Zell, two of the wildest boys on campus. "Janet, come on! I see our boys!

"Bye, Tommy!" She waved. The girls grabbed their purses and headed out to play.

"Janet, wait, I got a guy I want to introduce you to!" A light bulb went off in Tommy's head as he thought of my dad.

"Have him write a letter of introduction to my mom, Belle Conley, in Garrett, KY!"

"Right." Tommy shook his head and waved at the girls, already down the street. Just a beat or two later, a good-looking young man walked into the bar.

"Bill, I was just thinkin' of you buddy!" Tommy liked regular customers like Bill. He was still young at twenty-six and not as wild as the college crowd, but he wasn't ready for the grandpa booth either.

"What's playing?" Bill looked at the jukebox, still full force with 10 songs to go. He turned back to situate himself at the bar, and suddenly stood up again. "And who made these footprints?"

"Ah, a college cutie was dancing on the bar just now, even left a souvenir," he replied, pointing to the distinctive little feet patterns along the entire length of the bar.

"You don't say. I'd like to meet her."

"She told me she's looking for a real man...maybe she'll make an exception for you!"

"Ha. I just remembered I'm on the soon-to-be-divorced diet, Tommy. No women in my foreseeable future."

"Suit yourself, but I'm telling you she's gorgeous. Blonde hair, about five foot four, a shape that keeps on coming, and dances like a minx, as you can see." Tommy started pouring Bill's drink, and then leaned over the bar. "No kidding, Bill. You should meet her." He had a hunch, and being a bartender, he had learned his hunches were usually right on the money.

Bill took a sip of his scotch and slapped the bar. "Okay, I'll marry whoever made those footprints. How's that for a gamble?"

"That's a bold move. You might want to start with her name. It's Janet," Tommy reported.

"Janet. I like it."

"You gotta get permission from her mom!" They both laughed.

A year later, Bill was valet parking his car at The Little Inn nightclub in Lexington with his friend Walter White in tow. They were both young and handsome. Nights out at the "it" club were standard for the dynamic duo...lady linking as they went. Both good old boys from Cincinnati, they'd also seen life from the dark side as WWII vets. After serving their country, they had earned the right to live it up and they were making the most of it. Tonight they were going stag.

The atmosphere of dancers, gabbers, and drinks never got old. Surrounded by swing music and beautifully dressed couples, they found their usual table in the corner of the swanky club. The moment they sat down, a smart-looking cocktail waitress in a short black dress and fishnets made a beeline for the guys. She struck a stance.

"Betty!" Walter exclaimed, apparently a tad smitten.

"Hi, Bill..." Betty batted her eyelashes at the dashing frequent customer, "Scotch and soda on the rocks?"

Walter looked at her with a pout.

"Bets, Johnnie Walker on the rocks for me and the same for Walt. Any chance you have that Chef's Special goose pate tonight?" Bill knew just about every club owner and headwaiter in town.

"I'll have him make it up special...just for you."

"Why, thank you, dear. You look ravishing tonight." Bill tipped his fedora and set it on the small table.

Betsy practically tripped making her way back to the kitchen, bashing through the double doors.

"You devil." Walter winked.

"I'm just ordering...where's Agnes?" Bill inquired.

"In Fresno with rat fink. The sooner she's remarried the better." Walter's wife of five years had left him for another man.

"Gotta divorce first," Bill pointed out.

"Look who's talking."

They laughed. My dad was separated from his wife, their union a casualty of the unavoidable distance of war. Dad had been trying to finalize the divorce for a few years, but it was tied up in the Fayette County court system with a rigid female red-headed judge who seemingly didn't take kindly to breakups...or men for that matter. Despite the setback, Dad shook it off and returned to the hustle and vibe of hot jazz playing and the beautiful people dotting the low-lit club. It reminded him of the film *Casablanca*. If he looked hard enough, he might see Humphrey Bogart dealing out passports in a corner somewhere.

Then a drum sound with a snappy jungle-like beat roared through the club. Bill felt the urge to hit the dance floor, tapping his foot to the music.

"Who's that?" Walter turned his head almost clear around like a startled owl. Balanced on top of a table behind them was a gorgeous blonde in a tight black dress, gyrating to the music while holding her heels in one hand and sipping a Martini in the other.

"It's 'Footprints!'" Dad's eyes grew big.

"What?" Walter was a bit confused.

"It can't be..." Dad had a flashback of the bar top.

"You won't believe this, but Tommy told me about a girl who danced at the Jolly Trolley over a year ago. I never found her."

"She didn't have a phone?" asked Walter.

"I was supposed to write a letter of introduction to her mother before courting her. Too bad I didn't have her address. That's how it's done, apparently."

"In 1776," Walter shouted after him as Bill made a beeline over to Janet.

Janet looked down mid-sip to see a good-looking man extending his hand out to her. "You're the one!"

"Well, thank you," Janet cooed as she gracefully stepped down. "Exactly which one am I?"

"I'm Bill."

"Hi, Bill," she smiled sweetly.

"Are you by any chance Janet?"

"Uh, yes. I am. And you are a handsome devil!" Janet was not new to the flirting game.

"And you're the girl who made those footprints on the bar a year ago at the Jolly Trolley. Tommy told me all about you."

"I could be. I dance on a lot of tables!"

"I see that. Where *don't* you dance on the tables, my dear?"

"At wakes! Oh, wait a minute I've done a few of those, too!"

Dad was anxious to see if she remembered. "Tommy said that I needed to write a letter of introduction to your mother first, so…"

"Oh my! Yes! Hey! Why didn't you ever write?" she laughed, shaking his hand. "Bill, it's a pleasure to finally meet you!"

The couple chatted through the next three songs, entranced, until the music changed from the brassy beat to a rhumba.

"Can you rhumba, Janet?"

"I can sure as hell try!" Bill loved her moxie and abandon. He led Janet to the dance floor and they were in sync immediately, like magic, and danced divinely for years to come.

As they casually strolled back to their table, Bill whispered. "Janet, may I take you home tonight?"

"Well, you're going to have to ask my sister." She waved at the beautiful Rita a few tables away.

"Ah yes…I already have." Bill surprised her.

"Oh, a man who plans ahead. And what did she say?"

"She said it was ok." Bill raised a glass to Rita who was watching the whole interchange. In the charm department, Janet had met her match. My father was handsome, well-mannered, and expressed himself beautifully.

"Well, we better make sure. And Walter?" Janet questioned.

"He's a big boy."

Walter stepped up to the couple, "I'm the one who spotted you first, Janet."

"I've been waiting for you for a year, darling," Bill said. Janet smiled and took the boys arm and arm and introduced them to Rita and their entourage.

After a few minutes, Rita smiled and nodded at the couple.

"Well, Bill, I'll let you take her home on one condition: that you go straight there, and we will meet you in thirty minutes."

Bill happily agreed and assured Rita that he would take excellent care of my mother.

"Bill, I don't usually go home with strangers, but you look like Tyrone Power, so I'll trust you, darlin'."

"Oh, not Robert Taylor?" Bill and Janet walked to the valet stand.

"Him too! And how did you get such curly eyelashes? Do you use an eyelash curler?"

It was becoming apparent to Bill that looks weren't the only virtue in Janet's arsenal. He was enjoying that childish *je ne sais quoi* about her, even though he was ten years older than our little vixen.

Much to Janet's dismay, an indistinguishable gray Plymouth drove up to the valet booth a few minutes later. Dad held the door for her, being the gentleman he was. Against basic instinct, she got in the car anyway.

After the shock of not getting into at least a Mercedes, Janet realized they had a lot to talk about, with no awkward date moments and plenty of laughs. They carried on like two kids after school, taking the long way, of course, back to the University of Kentucky campus.

The bright streetlights guided the couple past old antebellum homes and large oaks along Governor Street, finally winding around to 130 Leader Avenue.

"Janet, may I call you?" Bill asked as he approached the driveway. "I don't want to wait another year, unless you want to tell me your class schedule, and I'll see what other chance meetings we might have."

"Yes, you can call," Janet said. "However, just as friends. You're still married and I'm not that kind of girl."

Dad smiled. "I understand. That's fine." Bill stopped in front of the huge white house and turned to kiss Janet on the cheek.

Janet dodged it and shook his hand. "And don't wear that silly fedora next time!" She took the hat off and tossed it in the back seat, revealing his dark, wavy hair.

"I'll never wear a hat again, my dear," he promised.

Over the next few months, Bill and Janet talked constantly, until Janet invited him "down home" to meet Belle and Warren Conley. The visit was a success. (The brothers even asked him when he was changing his name to "Conley." Sound familiar?) Belle was also a little smitten with Bill, especially his penchant for starched white shirts and good manners. He was certainly no local yokel from "the Holler." He was citified and educated with an engineering degree from the University of Cincinnati and a war veteran to boot.

"He's a well-dressed gentleman, Janet. I like him," Belle declared with her stamp of approval. However, Belle did have one reservation, and it was a big one. No divorce, no Janet.

"But Mrs. Conley, I've tried and tried," sighed Bill. "The judge won't grant it."

"No problem, Bill. We'll look into it for you. I can't have my Janet running around with a married man. It just wouldn't be right." The next day Belle and Warren "made a call" to the judge and immediately started the ball rolling. Walter finished the process by handing it off to his cousin, the judge, and Bill was divorced in just one month.

He and Janet were married two years later in the University of Kentucky Chapel—Rita and Robert, who eventually married, served as witnesses. The handsome couple was bursting with excitement and anticipation for a future together. Bill was ecstatic to have not only met but also married the woman he had heard so much about from Tommy at The Jolly Trolley. What he didn't know was that Janet had been planning this coup for years. Of course she didn't know exactly who he would be, but she knew her husband would be older, refined, educated, not wild and reckless, but most importantly, ambitious.

Janet had imagined this scenario over and over as she watched the movie news of the latest celebrity marriages in 1952 amid glaring flashes of the cameras and dazzling red carpets. She wasn't sure exactly what her future held, but she knew one thing. There would be promise—promise of a life beyond the confining mountains of Kentucky—where she could explore the dreams that had danced in her head for years. There had certainly been some hiccups along the way, but for the most part, her life was going as planned. Janet was ready to unleash her potential into the world, darling!

Bill knew that his new bride was ambitious, hell, everyone knew that. In fact, he knew she was more ambitious than he was. It was part of the reason he was so damn attracted to her. She was always the center of attention and the person everyone wanted to be around. That made him proud…and maybe a little anxious. Behind that beautiful exterior, he was never really sure what she was thinking. He only knew that he'd better be prepared for anything. He just hoped the rest of the world was ready, too.

# Chapter 7: Active Flush

*A star's a star, dear!*

It was a misty day in Detroit and Janet was anxious about her first out-of-town gig, the Home Show in Chicago at the famous Merchandize Mart. She had landed this prestigious job with renowned millionaire playboy Ozzie Hogan, head of the Driscol Plastics Empire. Ozzie was such a womanizer that he had a new model "host" his suite of prestigious guests while on the road every day of the week. According to most of the girls, each model was required to give Ozzie more than 100 percent if they wanted the job.

And Janet was his newest project.

She arrived at the airport in her long black sweater dress, side cape, Dior heels, belt and purse to match, short veiled pillbox hat (naturally with matching hatbox), long black leather gloves, her hair quaffed, makeup perfect, smelling of her notorious Chanel No. 5 perfume, wearing pearl earrings, a pearl necklace, and a pearl ring that she fancied would operate as her poison potion dispenser if she got into a fix. Move over, Jean Patchett! What a vogue vision!

Being late for the plane was not unusual for Janet, as she ran in her heels on the tarmac as fast as her fitted dress would allow. With a final boost of energy only name brands could give, she propped her luggage, hatbox and all, up on the top steps of the small private plane where Ozzie sat reeking of Glenfiddich scotch.

"Come on in, Janet," said the 40ish, very tall man as he checked his gold Rolex watch slowly, waiting for her to notice the impressive timepiece.

Janet steadied herself by the closet door upon entering the plane in a dramatic gesture, hand over her brow. "I just ran the Olympic mile! Next time, park at the terminal!"

"Here's your Martini, Janet. Next time I'll use the valet." he handed her a drink.

"Ha, touché! This will help!" They toasted and he gave her a polite kiss on the cheek. So far, so good. Janet noticed there were no other passengers on the plane, and waved to the pilot. "This is my first Chicago gig, Captain dear, so please don't screw it up for me now!" She smiled as she touched his shoulder lightly.

"Roger," shouted the pilot. There were chuckles in the cockpit.

She grabbed another Martini from a nearby tray and sat down next to the big man. "What a morning!"

"Janet, it's great to have you here." Ozzie slapped his big meaty hand down on her thigh.

Janet slowly moved it to his armrest. "Ah, ah, ah…" she scolded. "A girl's gotta keep focused on the job."

"Oh, didn't I tell you the specifications?" He smiled.

"You did. I'm working the toilet section. What's my speech?" she picked up his briefcase.

Ozzie grunted quietly and reached into his briefcase to hand Janet the booth spiel that had been prepared for her. She began to read immediately, before the alcohol took hold.

"How does it sound?" he asked.

"Hmmmm…very convincing…active flush?"

"Definitely, high tech." He nodded proudly.

"Of course!" she raised her glass. "To active flush!" They clinked glasses.

While keeping Ozzie's hands occupied with drinks, Janet raved about the job and the trip. Just for good measure, she mentioned Bill and the possibility of having a baby. "I'm really thinking about it, Ozzie." She paused a second to look out the window at the billowy clouds, thinking here she was once again at a crossroads, deciding which path to choose. While this was certainly a smaller job than some of the previous offers, it still required her to keep a slim figure, something she wasn't guaranteed after childbirth. Her introspection was soon interrupted.

"So am I!" He laughed and pawed at her again.

"Oh BAD BOY!" She slapped his wrist and laughed hysterically, hoping to dissuade him once and for all.

When they landed at O'Hare, Janet waved to the airport employees like she was Jackie Kennedy stepping down from Air Force One. She was whisked away in a cab to the bar at the Whitehall Hotel where Ozzie routinely situated his "models" every week. Janet walked into the hotel bar to find six other women, all gorgeous and charming, but, she conceded, not really with that "it" factor. Happy to pass Ozzie off on another more willing woman, Janet scanned the Ritz bar and thought to herself, *Now, this is more like it.* Looking at the well-heeled customers, she just knew that deals were being made and money was changing hands. The atmosphere was positively electric.

These trips were important to Janet because being the wife of a salesman could be very lonely. Her only real connection to the outside world was TV or the newspaper. On gigs like this one, she couldn't wait to soak in the local culture, and see first-hand how business was done outside of Detroit. She was determined to make these trips about much more than just waving her hands over a product all day. She wanted to make contacts, meet new people, be part of the action, and propel her career.

Each model ordered something petite when it came to dinner that night, mostly Waldorf salads and carrot sticks. Janet, however, wanted a burger. And what better way to impress her new boss than order it in French.

"*Je veux une hamburger, s'il vous plait!*" She threw up her arm in a grand gesture.

Ozzie opened his jaw. "Janet! You speak French!"

"You know it, darling! *Oui, oui.*" She smiled.

The bar band started playing. Her natural inclination was to jump up and start dancing on the table, but this time she held back a bit. She was on a job and part of that responsibility was to be...refined.

"I'm so impressed. You are going to be the hostess in my suite on opening night!" Ozzie traditionally hosted major celebrities in his suite after the Home Show ended. It now was even less clear if the modeling job was in his executive suite or in the Merchandise Mart, but Janet saw opportunity and squealed with delight.

"Oh, Ozzie, *merci beaucoup!*" She toasted the table, the other girls glaring back at her.

The next night, as predicted, after a successful show the celebs hit up Ozzie's suite. There was Mayor Daley, columnist Irv "Kup" Kupcinet, and even Frank Sinatra who was performing at Mr. Kelly's that night. Janet had aced her hostess duties. She knew how to work a crowd. No sooner had the gentlemen sat down when Janet appeared beside them, drink in hand, with a cocktail weenie chaser at the ready. Ozzie was truly impressed with her grace, poise, and ability to talk to anyone...no matter what background or social status.

"Oh, Kup, tell me, is it true?" She struck an inquisitive pose on the sofa, not entirely sure what was being discussed but certain she should interject something.

"I don't know what you mean, Janet." He looked at her, perplexed. She thought quickly. "Well, is it?" She leaned in.

"Uh..."

"I hear you're the best columnist since...Oscar Wilde!" she burst out, "or someone famous like that. Fascinating work!"

"Well, thank you..." Kup nodded his head focusing more on her beauty than her words.

"Mr. Mayor! Have a shot of this!" She poured a pink substance in his champagne glass. "It's cham...borg."

"Why thank you." Mayor Richard J. Daley smiled. He seemed fascinated with the beautiful redhead.

"I voted for you," she whispered when she got closer to him.

"Oh, excellent, where in Chicago do you live?" asked the mayor.

"Um, in the middle, of course," Janet cooed.

"Oh, very good." He nodded and motioned her over to his circle of guests. Janet was, at last, in her element, hobnobbing with the rich and famous. Not a care in the world.

"Hey, Janet!" Her manager, Stan, jumped between the celebs and gave her a big hug.

"Stan!" Janet said with a start. Stan was a plain-looking guy, not quite her class, she thought, but…given the circumstances she was glad to have someone there she trusted. He'd been her manager for two years and he'd gotten her this gig so she figured he was checking up on his account.

He whispered, "Janet, I'm going to do an errand…I'll be back. When's the end of your shift?"

"Ozzie said 9:00 p.m.," she whispered back.

"I'll be back at 8:00 p,m. Don't trust him," Stan warned.

"Oh, you really think he's all that bad?" Janet sipped her Martini and widened her eyes a tad. He gave her a stern look. "All right, silly." She knew better. Stan had always been a good friend, with somewhat of a crush on her, something she was certainly used to.

Ozzie jumped in. "Stan, wow, you have a beautiful client here…my new star—"

"In home improvement." Stan finished his sentence.

"A star's a star, dear." interjected Janet.

"And she is. Gorgeous. Knocked it out of the park this afternoon and tonight!" Ozzie put his arm around Janet's waist. "Darling, I want you to meet someone."

They all turned around.

Janet just about buckled her knees…Stan caught her drink.

"Mr. Sinatra," Janet managed.

"Hello, doll." Frank Sinatra was much smaller in stature than Ozzie, but had a presence you just didn't mess with. "Ozzie's in love with you. When's the wedding?" He smiled, sipping his scotch.

"Oh really, that's so sweet." Janet blushed. The thought of being married to such a powerful man was intoxicating.

"Tonight!" Ozzie laughed.

"Well, warm up for my show's in ten minutes at Mr. Kelly's— backstage passes for everyone…even you, Stan." Sinatra turned for the door.

"Thanks, Frank."

"Don't mention it." Sinatra turned and pointed his finger at Ozzie, half seriously. "And don't mess up, I like this one. "

"Thanks a million, Frank." Ozzie gulped.

"See you all there." He winked at Janet.

"You were a hit, honey." Ozzie was genuinely was impressed with not only with her work, but the way she handled herself in front of a true celebrity.

"Thanks, Ozzie, really, what an amazing time we're having." Janet sighed thinking he may not be so bad after all.

"Ok you two…" Stan stepped in between them, "keep it all business and I'll be back in an hour."

"Kill joy!" Ozzie sneered.

"That's my job, Ozzie." Stan turned and left.

"Bye, Stan!" The next hour, more Chicago notables dropped in and Janet charmed them all. She was in seventh heaven.

Meanwhile my dad was in Des Moines, Iowa, at a chemical plant closing a deal for Warner Electric, his own kind of excitement.

"Sandy, you got a phone around here? My wife's in Chicago with the biggest SOB I've ever seen. Gotta check on her." Bill grabbed his coffee and took a sip. Their engineering and sales teams had been working most of the night. Dad participated on both, being an engineer.

"You got it, Bill. I got the company plane all gassed up and ready just in case," said Dan Brock, one of his associates. Dan was actually from Chicago and knew Ozzie through deals he'd participated in a few years ago.

"So you know Ozzie, huh?" Bill lit a cigarette.

"Yeah…and I know Janet. She'll kick him in the nuts." Dan laughed.

Later that night Dad tried her hotel room. No answer.

Back in Chicago-star-paradise, Janet caught her reflection in the glass coffee table and realized her lipstick may not be perfect, practically a cardinal sin in her profession.

"Oh!" she exclaimed, truly afraid her star status would be a risk with less lip liner. She quickly grabbed her purse. "I gotta run to the ladies. Which way?"

Ozzie pointed to the bedroom. "Just through there, honey."

Janet rushed to the ornate gold-gilded bathroom, concentrating on lip liner when a large hand grabbed her from the back, landing on her breast. She jumped.

In one swift move, Ozzie lifted tiny Janet and plopped her at the foot of the bed just as the doorbell sounded.

"Humph!" Ozzie fumed.

Janet squirmed out of his arms and ran out of the bedroom to open the door. "Stan, darling!" She then whispered, "Ah, just in time."

"Hey, Stan," Ozzie offered when he eventually came out of the bedroom. "You got some timing."

"It looks like the guests have gone, Ozzie. Janet's got a big day tomorrow. Come on, honey," he held up Janet's jacket.

"Yes, Ozzie. Gotta run! Thanks and see you tomorrow." She grabbed her purse and faked a smile. They walked far down the hall and punched the elevator button. "Stan, you saved me. What a beast!"

"I should have never sent you on this gig, but I figured I'd be able to watch him. Sorry, Janet."

"It's okay, Stan. Comes with the territory. I've been dealing with guys like that all my life."

The next morning Janet found Ozzie's corporate headshot, sketched a caricature of it, and during the height of the show, made an announcement with everyone there. "And now, I'd like to present our fearless leader, the President of Driscol Plastics Enterprises and the CEO of American Home Furnishings, Mr. Ozzie Hogan!" She went over to the toilet display on the wall and lifted the lid to show her drawing of Ozzie smiling inside the frame of a toilet seat for the entire convention to see.

There was a hush over the crowd. Janet wasn't sure how he would take it, but she was willing to risk it. If nothing else, it would send a message. Everyone looked at Ozzie, red faced, with his hand to his mouth. After a nanosecond, which seemed like an eternity to the young model, he laughed a loud, forced laugh.

"Isn't she something?" Ozzie finally spoke out. The crowd laughed along with him.

"You look good in porcelain, Ozzie!" a guy in the crowd yelled out.

"Thanks." He held a fake smile.

After the show, Ozzie slowly made his way to the stage and helped Janet down.

"You going to fire me, Ozzie?" Janet put her hands on her hips.

"No, I was an ass. I'm sorry, Janet," he said.

"I'll let it go, *this time*," she scolded.

She never told my dad about what happened or how many of those "close calls" she actually endured during her modeling career. She slowly began to realize that her hunger for power and money, at least on this trip, wasn't all she had hoped, well, except for meeting Ol' Blue Eyes. Bill greeted her at the airport and she was genuinely glad to see him, eager to put the adventure behind her.

"Did Stan watch out for you?" Bill knew Stan had a crush on Janet, but he was used to it.

"Yes, thank goodness. I truly couldn't have done it without him," Janet replied.

"Any moves from that creep?"

"Ozzie is fine, Bill. You never have to worry about that kind of thing," Janet said, trying to reassure him.

"I know he is. Sweetheart, let's keep the modeling around town from now on, okay?"

"Well...okay, darling," Janet answered, reluctantly. She was actually relieved that she wouldn't have to face that type of situation again, one where she was alone and vulnerable. If it was between her husband and her career, she knew what she had to do.

So Janet only agreed to regional assignment after that. She was featured in the local newspaper, walked in fashion shows, and even toyed with a job offer on a TV show. All of those things were exciting, but she had decided that her main focus would be on her husband and the baby she was expecting. It was a decision she would always wrestle with. When I came along, I was, and am, the reminder of what could have been.

It was a tough way to grow up, I can tell you that. Despite the fact that her choice had been made, I couldn't help but feel guilty, just as I did when I would flip through her old pictures or listen as she shared stories with other couples while I eavesdropped from the hallway in my pajamas.

So maybe because of that, because I was one of the reasons for the choices she had made, I was eager to win her approval. I was willing to dress as she instructed, participate in activities she advised me to, and try to shoehorn my personality into her unrequited future (at least until my teen hormones made me a bit of a rebel). If I could follow in her footsteps, it would bring her the happiness she felt that she missed out on. And if I were successful, she would be so proud of me.

Perhaps I was being too dramatic, but I don't really think so, especially since she managed to deliver that basic message to me, in one form or another, almost every day of my life: whether she wanted me to associate with rich kids or put on my makeup and lip liner whenever I went out in public.

Fame was indeed everything for The Daily Janet.

# Chapter 8: White Gloves and Party Manners

*Do everything in heels, Ladies!*
*Life looks better when you're three inches higher.*

By the 1970s, our family had a model auto executive home in the upper middle class suburbs of Detroit called Huntington Woods. While not quite the money of an Iacocca or Ford, Janet and Bill had made a charming life for themselves in a lovely brick home only a stone's throw away—or three miles, to be exact—from the Detroit border and the race riots of 1967. Janet had naturally decorated our house herself, designing the living room as a replica of the Versailles Palace, complete with Louis XVI chairs, overly ambitious crystal chandeliers, and candelabras that would have made Liberace jealous. The floors were black-and-white tile and we owned what was said to be the first yellow-dyed carpet in town. Believe it or not, having light-colored carpet was very trendy and considered to be quite a statement in the cloistered community. Seriously, it was a big deal. There wasn't a carpet like it in the state of Michigan. In the '70s, upholstery was usually brown, plaid, or some shade of igneous rock.

As a young girl, I was treated much like our designer home and adorned with every Saks Fifth Avenue outfit Janet could find, right down to my Givenchy tasseled shoes. She dressed me like her own life-size doll, despite my protests. At first it was a bit flattering to receive so much of Mother's attention and as I've mentioned, I soon realized that it was sometimes at the expense of our relationship. The time we spent together wasn't to build a bond, but to create a showpiece, something to parade in front of adoring neighbors, friends, and business associates. To that end, I was enrolled in White Gloves and Party Manners, an organization designed to instill young ladies with culture, etiquette, and other crucial life skills such as to always cross my legs, one in front of the other, while sitting down, and especially when being photographed.

As a wife and mother, Janet's modeling career was now little more than memories on the walls and stories over a few strong drinks. So, being the socialite and fashionista she was, Janet channeled her energies into entertaining and regaling guests with tales of her brushes with stardom. Soon she found herself hosting one elaborate shindig after another. Events featured a private performance with a section of the Detroit Symphony, fire-eating gypsies, world-class pianists, music conductors, belly dancers, and local celebrities and politicians. Nothing was too outrageous for the enterprising young woman behind the man.

This was the era when three-Martini lunches sealed a deal with little more than a handshake. Janet was in her element as the perfect hostess, and Bill realized that clients were fascinated by her charming stories and her ability to keep any crowd entertained. She was the belle of the ball with a cigarette holder in one hand and a Martini shaker in the other, working the room like a pro using her signature leg kick at every turn.

Holidays were definitely a call to action, and that action, like with her theater group, was to party. On Thanksgiving, Janet instituted the annual Thanksgiving Belly Dance whereby she'd shake her booty and even hop up on the coffee table to a stunned audience, just like she had done years ago at The Jolly Trolley. This time she was much classier with a shimmery veil, gold bracelets, metal castanets for clanging and gold-tasseled Dior pasties—yes, pasties—and used her gyrating hips to challenge family values with a bump and a grind as I accompanied her on the tambourine. Dad would often be on the bongos with theatre friends while Aunt Fee Fee (whose 1969 breast implants were made from silicon and often the subject of careless whispers) played the cymbals. Our beloved Uncle Chester (one of the first publically openly gay man in Michigan) volunteered to jump in if she needed backup. It was quite the scene.

"Hit it, Bill!" Janet positioned her hips and gave a "hello" shake in the midst of confused auto execs, awaiting her cue to start shaking to the Arabic tune *Port Said*. The drooling husbands hooted and hollered while jealous wives fussed with the turkey baster and checked on the squash casserole.

Ah, family traditions.

My mother was deceptively clever. She sometimes came off as a carefree partier only concerned with when her next Martini would be ready, but there was always more behind her actions. She knew that the wives and girlfriends talked about her, being sweet to her face and doing a 180 when her back was turned. However, this wasn't her first rodeo. She had been dealing with girls like these starting with cheerleading and on up to her modeling career. I wouldn't categorize her as spiteful, but sometimes, just to make a point to a jealous, mean-spirited wife, she'd contact the office of one of the prominent party guests.

"Hello, McArthur, Ramsey, and Redon, can I help you?"

"Oh hello, is Frank there?" asked Janet.

"Frank...?"

"Oh, I think it's Frank Smith..."

"You mean Frank Sears?"

"Sure, that's the one. Yes, would you tell Frank that he left his watch here and to call Janet..."

She knew the nosy receptionist would likely waste no time calling Frank's wife to verify she knew of his whereabouts the previous evening.

It should come as no surprise that our house was one of contradictions: A sculpted bust of Kennedy rested high on a Doric pedestal in the foyer despite the fact that my parents voted Republican. Party affiliation aside, Janet was attracted to the dynamic and handsome US President and enamored not only by Jackie's beauty, but her tremendous style—the power couple was the epitome of what she wanted her life to be. Yet, while you may not see Jackie Kennedy partying in the Blue Room quite like Janet in her Huntington Woods "Yellow Room," the two did share some fashion similarities: the oversized sunglasses, Chanel tailored suits, pillbox hats, gloves, Yves St. Laurent capes and of course all matching accessories (like most women of good standing).

While I was too young to be a part of their lively social life, I was certainly in awe of it, and especially of my beautiful mother. I saw the way she worked a room, how she handled the drunken men and delicately schooled the catty ladies. I remember thinking how amazed I was by her, but how it also made me a little sad. It was clear even to a little girl like me that this wasn't where she had hoped to be in her life. Sure she was making the most of it, and she was doing a great job, but the times were a-changing. Women's lib was pushing its way into our national lexicon, thanks to that incessant song by Helen Reddy.

I knew by the way she literally groomed me to be like her that I would be her second, and last, chance. She was pinning those dreams, her dreams, on me, her only child. And for a while I did enjoy the attention because I saw that everyone wanted that from her, and she was giving it to me. And the more I tried to fit into the mold she was creating for me, the less comfortable I felt. I needed to first figure out who I was and what I wanted. Maybe we would agree and maybe not.

It was a lot of pressure and I felt it every day. I constantly found myself wrestling with pleasing my mother and being true to myself. Anytime I pushed back, I could feel her resentment and anger...even rage. I wanted to please her, I really did. I loved it when she paraded me around, so proud of her little creation, but it never felt genuine or truly loving.

I quickly learned how to self-manage my feelings, my expectations, and my dreams. If I pushed back too much, it just created conflict and I didn't want that. I loved it when my mother was happy and carefree and fun. The only problem was that I had to give up who I was in order to get that from her—something that didn't register with her. She was not good with compromise, and I knew that. So I went along with most everything she suggested and it worked...

Until it didn't.

# Chapter 9: Dior and Demons

*Children are to be seen by a movie producer and not heard until you let them out of their room.*

Kindergarten was a hallmark year. I had perhaps the most frustrated of women as a teacher, Mrs. Harry . What made matters worse than her screaming at my slow-learning, later-to-be-diagnosed-as-dyslexic ways was what preceded it every day, Janet getting me ready for school.

My father was always out of town on a sales call and was essentially gone throughout my early years. Maybe he planned it that way. I don't know for sure. With him being out of the picture, Janet basically had the task of raising me and part of that meant dressing me for school. It started when I was five years old and I quickly came to dread each day. I knew it would begin slowly and then quickly escalate into ranting and yelling.

"Where is your Calvin Klein dress? Where is it? Where is it?" Janet paced back and forth in her robe in the hall, grabbing her head, possibly slightly hung over from the previous night's social event.

"In the closet," I said and pointed. I was sitting on my bed, trying to pull on my tights.

"You little smart ass. Don't talk back to me!" She stood in the doorway of my bedroom, as if she were ready to spring on me. She was an imposing figure when she wanted to be. I knew to talk would mean more of the same.

Silence.

With one swift jerk, Mom pulled the tan wool knit dress off the hanger and roughly pulled it over my little body. It scratched my skin, but I did not dare say a word. My lip was stiff and my dark circles were wet with tears.

"What are you crying about?"

"You," I answered.

"Me?" She put her hand on her hip. "You're crying about me, are you? After I've given you everything, done everything, sacrificed everything for you and your father! And you can't even hold still. Why, in my day…" She grabbed my shoulder and roughly pulled a brush through my long brown hair, seeming to relish when it tore my scalp, getting angrier and angrier with every stroke.

I saw this scene play out in the French standing mirror behind her. I was like a petite doll, a hopeless figure totally overwhelmed by her manic anger. My dress was wet from my tears and she started dabbing my chest with tissue using so much force that I almost fell over.

"You're late." She threw the brush on the vanity and started to pull at her own hair in desperation. "You're late. Goddamit, how many times do I have to get you and your father up in the morning?"

I still couldn't talk. I knew I'd start crying full out.

"Where's your mother-fucking lunch?" Her voice boomed throughout the upstairs.

I didn't know if I was supposed to answer.

"Where is it?" She insisted I have some sort of logical answer when we were nowhere near the kitchen.

"Mom, you haven't made it yet," I said softly.

"'You haven't made it yet,'" she mocked, just waiting for me to respond.

"I can get it at school." I tried to come up with something halfway plausible.

"'I can get it at school,'" she mocked again. Her mascara from the night before made harsh lines under her eyes. Her pink quilted robe was stained and she tapped her fingernails inside the front pocket as if ready to jab them right through her thigh. I closed my eyes tight and thought about the beautiful pictures of my mother standing beside the newest model Ford or GM vehicle, her face angelic.

She grabbed a barrette from the vanity and began to position it in my hair. The walls of my room were covered in sickly pink-and-red rose-patterned wallpaper. I stared straight ahead. I tried to focus on that mesmerizing pattern, but a sharp pain on my temple brought me back.

"Stop moving!" She raised her hand up and I winced. "Stop scrunching your face! You would have to have inherited my stupid nose."

I was shaking, just from trying to hold still.

"Alright, downstairs!" she finally blurted out, pointing.

With that command, I quickly ran down the stairs to the kitchen, searching for my bag and homework so I could run out the door without a challenge. I knew the sooner I got out of the house, the sooner I could relax.

"Here!" She pushed my bags at me, and then bent down to tie my shoes and pull up my red tights.

I took the opportunity to grab my homework and make my way outside.

"Come back here, I haven't put on your raincoat yet!" She threw open the downstairs closet and started to search frantically for my tan Calvin Klein raincoat with beautiful tailoring, excessive camel panels, and red piping (way too sophisticated for a five-year-old). While I understood that what she made me wear each day was expensive, it didn't make a difference to me. The kids at school couldn't have cared less, in fact, I was teased for it, but Janet had to have things her way.

"I don't need it, Mom." I tried to get out of this one. I hated raincoats.

"What?" she screamed and dangled it in front of me. "You always need a raincoat and this one was $379!" I backed up towards the door.

"You get back here right now," she screamed moving towards me, brush tight in her hand. "Your hair is a mess now! Goddamit, why can't you stay neat and beautiful like Julie does?"

Julie was a very pretty girl in school and Janet was always quick to compare the two of us. I think it started when she realized Julie was quite popular, even at that young age, something she had expected from me since I came into this world.

"Bye, Mom!" I opened the door, hearing it swing wide behind me, and ran a few house lengths down our block.

It was a short distance to Burton Elementary. I usually met my friend, Lynn, and walked with her the rest of the way. That day I caught up to her, panting. "What's wrong with you?"

I didn't say anything. I was just surprised I didn't start hysterically crying.

"Why does your mom scream like that?" Lynn asked.

I was embarrassed to realize that my mom's criticisms were shared with passersby. I just shook my head and looked at the sidewalk. Several other groups of kids were gathering down at the crosswalk. Lynn casually changed the subject and we made it to school on time.

That year, I had homeroom teacher Mrs. Harry, an agitated, worn out, middle-aged mess of a woman. Unfortunately, Mrs. Harry did not take a shine to me and that only made matters worse. No matter how well-dressed and stylish Janet made me, it meant nothing to this woman. Like Mom, she had fiery red nails and a temper to match.

It was 8:00 a.m. and everyone was in their seat. The first lesson of the day was pretty simple: draw a pumpkin. Ok, no sweat. I instantly thought of the Great Pumpkin from the *Peanuts* cartoon. Should it really be orange? No…that's every pumpkin, my pumpkin needed to be green and purple. My pumpkin had to be great…with a magic carpet and curb feelers…a cool *chapeau* and glitter gloves, but with a distinct face that's all about the harvest. I took the paper with an outline of a pumpkin and drew huge horns, hands, a magic carpet, a dapper hat with shades for eyes, and a team of minion pumpkins, or "pumpettes," in the background.

After some quiet scribbling, everyone passed their drawing to the front of the class.

"Jimmy, yes. Nice pumpkin, place yours on the board." She nodded with glazed approval in her eye. Smug Jimmy, biggest "spaz" in class, put his orange mess of a pumpkin on the board.

"Andrea, lovely." She had colored it orange…in the lines perfectly, with a curly stem. One of those groomed self-assured girls you knew would be a trophy wife or a bitch marketing executive.

"Daniel, you could use more orange." She tried to make a small laugh that didn't quite go over. He had one orange line through it. Brilliant. She stopped and stared at the next piece of paper for what seemed like an eternity...she took a long deep breath. "What is this?" she said slowly. She turned the paper to the class and looked at me. "What is this, Leanna?" she said through clenched teeth.

"A pumpkin?" I said simply.

"IT'S NOT A PUMPKIN I HAVE NO IDEA WHAT YOU TURNED IT INTO. THAT WAS NOT THE ASSIGNMENT! PUMPKINS ARE NOT PURPLE WITH HANDS!" she literally screamed.

"Mine is," I felt totally justified in telling the truth.

"That's enough!" She made a grand gesture to sweep open the classroom door.

"OK."

"YOU! GO TO THE PRINCIPAL NOW!" She pointed her red-lacquered figure at me like a dagger.

I froze.

"GO!" She turned her head dramatically to the side as if fighting off something. Demons, apparently.

I slowly got up, the other kids seeming to relish the torment. Lynn gave me a look of sympathy and shrugged her shoulders. I walked alone down the green-lined hallway on my way to Principal Howe's office. I hesitated at the door. The secretary, Miss Dorsey, looked at me with surprise. I guess I was shaken because she rushed over to me and started to hug me.

"Honey, what happened?"

"I colored a pumpkin purple." I sniffed out the words.

Still not understanding, she said, "Aren't you supposed to be in class?"

"Mrs. Harry sent me here." My tone was neutral.

"For coloring something the wrong color?"

"I guess." I shrugged.

Mrs. Dorsey shook her head. "Ok, you stay with me for a while."

I colored quietly in her office and she asked if I was feeling well, how things were at home. Did she know what I went through every day? I was always paranoid that adults could tell, that they could somehow see through me and my secrets.

The next day did not bring a major reprimand as I had thought it would. Mrs. Harry was not as upset in fact, she didn't even look at me. So I don't know if Mrs. Dorsey said something or if my teacher was just over it. I also wasn't sure if my mother's reputation affected some of my relationships with teachers and other parents. Surely there was talk about her and her past as a (gasp) model, the word said with distain as if it was one-step removed from a streetwalker. And they knew Janet would have no problem letting them "have it" if need be.

As my school career progressed, I learned better how to deal with Janet. I loved when she was fun and playful, packing my lunch with party leftovers, sometimes even adding a decorative toothpick as a joke, knowing I liked to poke my food with it the way I saw them do at parties. And there were also times when she would come to my aid if someone threatened or treated me badly. Just like the protective Momma Lion she was. That was an advantage a lot of kids did not have and I knew it.

The dilemma for me was trying to figure out which mood she was in on any given day. It was almost like I didn't have the luxury of my own feelings. I only had a few split seconds each morning to assess how she was feeling and adjust accordingly, sometimes making a joke or funny face just to make it all right.

If I didn't, I knew there would be hell to pay.

# Chapter 10: Hot Dog Lunch

*You need mustard, darling. Nobody likes a plain boy.*

With her three-inch red heels, a matching Fendi bag, a black sheath dress, and hair coiffed into a chignon under her Givenchy picture hat, just like one Audrey Hepburn would wear to the races in *My Fair Lady*, Janet looked ready for Detroit's hot nightclub scene—except that she wasn't going clubbing. Janet's actual destination was the Burton Elementary fourth-grade class first-Wednesday-of-the-month Hot Dog Lunch—where the only "hot" was in the cooking temperature of the dog.

After working the brown-and-green Formica hallways like a catwalk in Paris, Janet finally found my class, Home Room 12. For me, the ten seconds after she opened the heavy door extended into an eternity. Everyone in the room stared, mouths open. One girl's sip of Pepsi actually dribbled down her chin and onto the ruffles of her dress.

Framed in the doorway, Janet was a *Vogue* vision: a redheaded bombshell with designer shades, a cascade of bracelets and pearls, and something metal in her hand she quickly slipped into her purse. (I also happened to know she carried orange Tang and vodka, for "emergencies," in a small silver flask, designer of course.)

Mrs. Beacon, the homeroom mother, seemed particularly puzzled about what to do next. I wanted to be a good daughter and say, "Hi, Mom," but the words stuck in my throat.

True to form, Janet was the one, of course, who had to "break the ice."

"Hello, darlings!" she boomed. "I'm ready for the hot dog lunch!"

Her laugh was infectious enough that a group sigh of relief passed over the room and the kids returned their attention to the silver-foiled hot dogs and buns that had been passed out just minutes before her arrival.

"Ah, Leanna's mother, I presume?" Mrs. Beacon said. I hung my head, not quite in shame, but from sheer confusion. *Should I be mortified or should I be happy she's here?* I combined my initial reaction with laughter to create a feeling of being "lortified"—laughing and mortified simultaneously—a new emotion I invented for the occasion. The kids immediately turned to look at me when they realized I was related, as in mother-and-daughter related, to this stylish vision. Those stares had to be the shortest stares on record because the whole class snapped their collective gaze back to Janet. (I was overshadowed by her even with my own classmates.)

Janet smiled and examined the room. "Well, this is charming." She quickly focused on Ricky Smith, the class nerd and a bit of a weakling, and headed right toward him.

*Uh oh.*

She picked up one of the mustard containers and said, pointing to the plain hot dog on this desk, "You need mustard, darling. Nobody likes a plain boy." She squeezed the bottle and buried the hot dog in the yellow sauce.

Stunned for a moment by her attention, Ricky sat transfixed and looked up in awe at the phenomenon before him. He squeaked out, "Okay," and began eating it, not seeming to mind the oozing yellow mustard all over his face.

Karen, my best friend, eventually became brave enough to send me a whisper. "You look nothing like her."

"Ya think?" I said, wiping my mouth after I gulped a big swig of Tab. I wasn't sure if that was a jab or a compliment.

Slowly, the chatter and noise of the classroom started up again and the other mothers regrouped and swung again back into action. They prepared the potato chips and coleslaw on Scooby Doo paper plates and napkins, and passed them out to the rest of the class. I could tell they were trying to ignore the dynamic, beautiful interruption that was surely interfering with their carefully planned monthly event.

From their jealous expressions, it was obvious they were not ready for my mother.

I tried not to focus on Mom and followed the lead of the room mothers—I would act like everything was fine. I'd had lots of practice. However, with my peripheral vision, I could see that she was trying to fit in, and once again I was conflicted. I appreciated that she was making an effort, but as was often the case, I could also see that it was useless. And, as usual, she was oblivious to that. She bellied up to the long serving table and struck a pose that feigned interest. And, whenever the conversation turned to cooking or sports, she forced a broad smile, trying her best to fit in.

"My Jimmy's in Little League," one mother said. "He's just a natural."

"Oh," retorted Janet, "Leanna's in Junior League." She started laughing wildly. After several more futile attempts at normalcy, she realized the room had gone quiet again. She was lost in a sea of blank faces. Janet walked over to my desk.

"Honey, this is the dullest party I've ever attended. But look how good your mommy is, eh?" She handed me a bag of chips and gave me a demonstrative hug. She flashed a fake smile, as if caught in a candid moment during a *Life Magazine* photo shoot at the Kennedy White House. "And here's some juice." She poured some of her spiked "Tang" into my Scooby Doo cup and took a swig of it. "I don't know how you stand coming here, day in and day out," she exclaimed, as if I had a choice. She turned to the rest of the class, "What a beautiful group of students. How well-dressed!"

As I shrank away from her, Seth Friedman stood up with a start, coughing and holding his throat.

"Seth's having an asthma attack!" Karen announced.

Seth clearly was in trouble, but it was not asthma. He produced gagging sounds that terrified all of us. His face went from white to red to blue. The whole class started screaming. Mrs. Beacon rushed over to help. Mrs. Sayer became so hysterical she spilled an entire tray of hot franks into the cage of Frankenstein, the class bunny. Only momentarily perplexed, Frankenstein started humping the franks to the delight of the class.

"Emergency! Emergency! Home Room 12!" cried Mrs. Beacon over the intercom system. Her voice boomed into every corner of Burton Elementary. Teachers and kids, hearing the dire school broadcast, came running in from all directions to see what was going on. The audience of would-be rescuers were soon helping themselves to whatever food they could get their hands on while watching the spectacle.

Taking it all in by the back window, Janet carefully touched up her lipstick and lit a cigarette. After a couple of puffs and a "once over" with her compact, she rushed over to Seth before anyone could stop her and got behind him, hitting his stomach, her red-nailed fist delivering a well-manicured Heimlich maneuver. Kids stared in disbelief, mouths agape. When that didn't work, she pulled him into her arms like she was dancing the tango and dragged him to the teacher's desk. She then administered mouth-to-mouth resuscitation right there in front of the classroom.

I started to pull my sweater over my head until I heard a burst of clapping. Seth opened his eyes and started to gasp for breath as Janet quickly pulled the piece of hot dog out of his mouth and threw it to Frankenstein. She then took a long drag off of her cigarette (which she had held on to tightly throughout the CPR process, an amazing feat when I stop to think about it).

She released the still stunned Seth and he dropped like a rock on the desk. *Clunk!* A few moments later, as the medics rushed in, Janet took a swig of her "juice."

"Well, hello, boys," she said as she eyed the two young paramedics.

For a couple of weeks after that I was known as the daughter of the lady in the big picture hat who had saved Seth's life. Janet had inadvertently given me a bit of schoolyard notoriety. Everyone knew who I was, and of course, who my mother was. There was much talk in the hallways about "that Janet lady who kissed Seth." (Apparently, Seth loved my mother's CPR so much he later became a chain smoker and Ricky was so smitten he grew up to become the youngest CEO in the history of French's mustard. Okay, not really…but it sounded good.)

Of course at the time I was horrified (*way* beyond lortified). Can you imagine that happening to you as a child? But looking back, it was nothing short of amazing. She had descended on my homeroom that day in an attempt to blend in, which I knew was futile. The other room mothers had basically ostracized her, but that didn't deter her. My mother has always had this uncanny ability to ignore the sneers and whispers of others. It is like her superpower. She is very secure with herself and I envy that unshakeable confidence—something that I have never quite been able to match in my own life.

I can now better appreciate my resourceful mom for not only saving the day, but doing it in stiletto heels, a tight dress, and clutching her modified astronaut juice.

For emergencies.

# Chapter 11: The Popularity Experiment

*Ladies, never underestimate the awesome power*
*of pure superficiality!*

There is a time in everyone's young life when your mom gets in the trenches of your day-to-day existence, and, as we know, Janet was a "butinsky" aficionado. Usually this takes place when you're going down the tubes because of sex, drugs, or poor grades. In my case it was much worse, a lack of fashion of sense. While Janet had spent most of my life dressing me like her designer paper doll, her push became more intense as I got older and started branching out into the wide world of public opinion.

I was twelve and attending Girl Scouts. I loved Brownies and Scouting, basically anything in uniform, for the very reason I did not have to concern myself with clothes, only an occasional barrette, underwear, and matching socks with shoes, and that alone presented a challenge with Janet presiding. I was not carrying the Revlon spokesmodel torch my mother had not-so-secretly hoped for. She saw the future of our relationship on the horizon, and it likely was not only *out* of season, it was never *in*. She'd lose her daughter to painter pants, mood rings, and Led Zeppelin cutoff t-shirts forever if she did not act quickly.

Janet also knew that next year her little non-fashion plate would be attending a private school, Kingswood School/Cranbrook in Bloomfield Hills, Michigan, which, unfortunately for me, had discarded the tradition of wearing uniforms that very year. Janet wanted to capitalize on the possibility that her daughter would one day become the fashionista, the star she always wanted her to be. And now was the time to mold her little prodigy. The future of fashion itself was literally hanging by a thread.

So Janet decided to give her daughter a taste of being popular and demonstrate the value of good looks and pure superficiality. She did the one thing she could: hop on board the bandwagon and become, yes, a Girl Scout badge mother. Not so bad for me. I figured that in Girl Scouts you wear a uniform with a sash over your shoulder and a snappy beret. Things were already looking up.

That Thursday, most of the "popular girls" were coming off of the school day loaded with gold stars. And they didn't disappoint when it came to badges. Their sashes were filled with colorful proclamations of success ranging from mountain climbing to pet rock grooming. I had one badge...the troop number. Janet was about to change that score once and for all.

Right in the middle of The Pledge of Allegiance, a big "humph!" hastily invaded our patriotism. Janet wore a fabulous Tahari suit, a beautiful caramel-colored scarf, matching gloves, and boots complete with a Girl Scout-style cashmere beret tilted just right. "Hello, darlings!" She struck her traditional pose, giving a disparaging once-over at the burnt-orange beanbag chairs and tie-dye curtains that adorned the dull gathering space. "Meet your new badge mother!" she kicked up her leg as a greeting, like an off-duty Rockette.

*Oh boy. Here we go,* I thought.

She then produced from under her cape a two-inch thick *Vogue* magazine with Jackie Onassis on the cover and immediately plunked it on the long stark folding table in the corner. "I even brought the new and improved Girl Scout manual!"

The troop leaders, Mrs. Jenkins and Mrs. Brown, looked at each other in amazement. Janet had managed to do the one thing she always did to perfection, render an unsuspecting audience speechless. Janet strutted through the room of gawking young girls, stopping midway to whisper an aside to the most obviously "loose" girl in the troop, Sheila Wains, sizing up her well-developed figure and excessive blue eye shadow with a disapproving shake of her head. "If I were you, I'd sleep with this by your side," she said, pointing to the Vogue magazine she just laid down.

Mrs. Jenkins finally managed to speak. "I think we have just the place for you, Janet," she said, shaking Janet's hand and smiling. Perhaps Janet was just the ticket for this Hobby Lobby hybrid of young girls—a Hollywood makeover for Troop 159! Let the games begin!

As far as fulfilling badge requirements, Mother was very strict with the troop. Of course, with me, I just put an "X" on a form and she'd send it to Girl Scout Grand Central and somehow a badge would magically appear two days later. I even accidentally burned a marshmallow in the parking lot and got the "science" badge. Yet, mysteriously, that year, I tied with Jennifer Jenkins (the most popular girl in the school) for the most badges. My sash was littered with stitched insignias and sewn round edges, overflowing with brightly colored patches. Oddly enough, the troop gave me more respect, thanks naturally to my mother's meddling. I could tell that she was very pleased with herself and what she had accomplished with her little popularity experiment.

Janet was such a bright shining light in this otherwise dull, traditional, suburban middle-class world. It made me wish, in a way, that she'd never had children, but rather had gone out to LA to be a star, to be a Revlon spokesmodel. Her wasted potential was so obvious I felt everyone could see it and perhaps that's one of the reasons why I found myself progressively retreating into the shadows. It was very clear to me that had I not been born, her potential would not be wasted managing my popularity status and progressively uncooperative attitude. Despite being embarrassed by her antics, I was so proud when she found success among the unwilling.

As I stood back in the corner of that once-somber meeting room watching Janet charm the girls and impress the leaders with her wit, and occasionally shocking them with inappropriate stories, I realized that even when she was a bit much to handle, when her anger got the best of her, she was operating with good intentions. Even in this environment—surrounded by weak fruit punch and Do-Si-Do Girl Scout cookies—I saw her amazing talent and ability to turn any situation around. It's a rare gift one that sometimes backfires. However, the resilient just dust themselves off and keep going, confident in their approach.

I didn't mind Janet taking all the focus and parading into the room at city hall that day, or most days for that matter. I admired her courage and strength of will. Janet was a force to be reckoned with. Even without the bright lights, she was a star. And, at this moment, as I looked down at my full sash, I was proud that she was my mother.

# Chapter 12: Fashion Affair

*Never let love get in the way of ambition,*
*or a good stiff Martini.*

If I haven't yet made it clear, while my mother had that love affair with fashion, to me designer clothes were just another way to suffer judgment from popular, brainless brats and mindless society queens. I clearly understood the "power of popularity" from my Girl Scout experience, but in my freshman year at Kingswood, the fight between "looks vs. substance" intensified. Reveling in my teenage rebellion, I hated designers and their labels, and I took every measure to sabotage the couture destiny Janet had planned for me. As it stood, I was living in the shadow of the glamorous fashionista, the bombshell model that all the boys wanted, including almost every "boyfriend" I dated.

Despite Janet's influence, or perhaps because of it, I preferred the anonymous world of sci-fi, fantasy, and J.R.R. Tolkien to real-life human phoniness, rampant hypocrisy, and exploited sensuality. I gladly accepted my fate. I was happy spending time alone, drawing horses, re-reading *Pride and Prejudice* and *The Hobbit*, playing with the only quasi-computer simulated game in town, Light Bright, alone in my dimly lit room. As an only child, I never knew anything else but being alone, so when I lost the companionship of a man I cared about in my later dating life—like biting into the apple of the tree of knowledge—I felt the difference, an emptiness I didn't realize I could feel.

Ignorance was indeed bliss.

So, as my teenage years began, I intentionally dressed down—no makeup, brown cords whenever possible—and even gave away my fancy clothes to less-fortunate kids any chance I got. In fact, I went as far as cutting the designer labels out of everything—goodbye Adrienne Vittadini and Givenchy. My closet was dotted with holes over the breast pockets of my Ralph Lauren tops and butt cheeks of Calvin Klein jeans. I was growing up and this was war. I was anti-commercialism, anti-conformity, and from her perspective, anti-Janet. And like two cage fighters at a smack down, it was coming to a head.

My room was the first battleground: half Madame Alexander dolls, half Spock posters and Breyer model horses. My closet, a "mish-mosh" of defiled clothes and strong wills. I slept in a canopy bed complete with frills, a lace and red rose-patterned bedspread, and wallpaper and drapes to match. It always reminded me of an ornate coffin. It was the room Janet had always wanted, but growing up as one of nine children, she never got it. So once again I was stuck with her dreams.

That year, Janet went into a major panic. She often mused aloud like I wasn't in the room: "What is Leanna going to be wearing to catch a rich man in college?" And, "how in the world will she work the room at a society cocktail party?" I was an enigma to her, and I could practically feel her confusion. She probably pictured my future as a mousey, drab librarian totally alone, poor and above all, tasteless. No. Not for her daughter, as God was her witness, Scarlett! Never!

Throughout my life, Janet would basically "lose her shit" when I wouldn't wear what she wanted or refused to look as she directed. She scrutinized me constantly, reminding me that I needed a nose job every morning and scolding me to put on more makeup "if I ever wanted to get a man." It was clear I did not align with her wishes and was not jumping on board the path she had envisioned for me since my stylish delivery in 1962. And, as the years passed, cooped up in the tame doldrums of suburban life, my ambitious talented mother, with no place else to channel her stellar energies, unraveled. I became good at dodging insults and avoiding her wild rants.

Then one day after school, Janet found my newest pair of Gloria Vanderbilt jeans hanging like a hostage on my bedpost with the label strategically snipped out of the arse. She looked into my closet to see the new line of mangled Dior and Anne Klein turtlenecks. She flew into a rage, throwing objects around the house wildly like a blind woman at a skeet shoot.

"Do you know how hard I work and sacrifice to make you what you are, you ungrateful bitch?" she shrieked at the top of her lungs.

For every absent label, a saucer would fly into the hallway. In two weeks we were out of dishes and it took practically a truckload of Spackle to patch the walls. Dad was getting worried. There was a price to pay for not satisfying his social-climbing wife with enough money and power, not to mention his humble influence on his daughter and their unmistakable bond. Then, the next morning, my *Saturday Night Live* Coneheads T-shirt was mysteriously shrunk to a doll's size and strategically placed on my bed.

"How do you like them apples?" Janet pointed at my shirt, hand on her hips.

Furious, I ran to her bedroom. I gathered her makeup and cigarettes, popped them into to our new blender, and frapped the thick colors into a lethal Chanel shake. Then I poured it into a Martini glass. After Janet saw it on the bar, I sprang to my room, her chasing me all the way up the stairs screaming at the top of her lungs, fists pumping in the air. Slam. Close call. I locked myself in my room to prevent further assaults. Janet beat on my door calling me out for what seemed an eternity.

Then it stopped.

I sat on my bed and cried. I was not good enough for this woman, this perfect beauty, and I never would be.

I needed new digs. I packed my bags several times that year, threatening to leave instead of attending private school with its new crowd of mean girls. But this time, it was for real. I couldn't risk the chance of staying in this house. If only I had been allowed to be me, not forced to live under her rules and tyranny and thigh-hugging Calvin Kleins (I came between my own Calvins, actually). I could not go out there to face her utter contempt. I had somehow become the enemy in our family home. As Janet predicted, Brooke Shields I was not. I was heavyset, drab, with braces, and to the flamboyant flirt and eternal party girl Janet, I was the ultimate disappointment.

That evening, after the atmosphere cooled, I made a break for it after watching re-runs of *The Avengers*. Emma Peel, the series' action heroine, oddly enough in a black cat suit, inspired me. I packed $100, all in quarters from my coin collection—well, why not? Immigrants say they make it in America on five bucks. I could do it in a week. I already spoke English. I would be a millionaire by fifteen. I had lots of teenage ambition and unchecked dreams.

But here I was with my fluorescent pink suitcase stuffed with *Star Trek* t-shirts, Butterfingers candy, and a lava lamp (for warmth). I snuck out the back door and rounded to the front of the house. The neighborhood was calm and still, the street lamps buzzing. A moment of quiet. Then I heard barking. The neighbor's sheepdog, Reggie, was definitely one of my favorite things about Huntington Woods, other than the Stevens boys who let me ride their trikes on dirt mounds and play their Rock'em Sock'em Robots. In the middle of innocently chasing Tiger, the cat from next door, Reggie stopped in his tracks and sensed the winds of change. Hair over both his eyes, he seemed to have a psychic capacity to navigate to food, Frisbees and, one of his favorite toys…me. When I was five, I was riding around on his back, using a clothes dryer sheet as a saddle, planning my rodeo debut in ruffled pants.

The big dog froze when he saw me, dropped the cat out of his mouth and bounded towards me.

"No, Reggie! Down!" I half-protested, falling backwards in the yard. Too late, he was already licking my face through his black and gray stringy hair. Love can really ruin your plans, I learned.

As I lay there, I realized how silly the situation was, and how appropriate. I was in no position to leave home and make it on my own, and it was very obvious, even to Reggie.

I tossed my bag into the bushes beside our house on Parkwood Drive and we trekked across the street to one of the many little parks in the Woods. I spent the rest of the evening tossing a Frisbee with the playful sheepdog away from makeup, clothes, and judgment. It gave me time to think, to put things into perspective. Maybe I was being too rash. I'd be going to college in no time and then I'd be on my own.

Janet wouldn't be there to push her ideas onto me, or live vicariously through me. She wouldn't be controlling my every move and teaching me how to be a lady.

And for a second I realized that I might just miss that.

# Chapter 13: The Popularity Coffin

*Pick a winner and you pick your destiny—that even goes for horses.*

It was a sleepy Sunday in Huntington Woods, fall 1977. The school year was in full swing, and we had already gotten my wardrobe, figured out the carpool situation, and selected my after-school electives at Kingswood.

The seasonal rain also brought one of the most humiliating experiences of my young life. I was a sophomore in high school, just old enough to know my place in its clique structure. I was what you call a nerd. Goth wasn't invented, but somehow it was similar to my look and feel, with a few '70s modifications like loose silk vests and tight velour headbands. Maybe I was a Goth hippie! (A Gippe?)

I wasn't unpopular, mind you, but my best friend was perhaps the heaviest girl in school. Everyone liked her, and my other bud was smart and pretty. But for some reason, we didn't really fit into any clique. Not enough money, not enough boys, too much *Star Wars*—whatever the case, I was definitely not in the jock/hottie group. I was more like an Ally Sheedy in *The Breakfast Club* wearing an occasional Molly Ringwald-inspired crop top for good measure.

Janet saw that I was comfortable in my decidedly specialized niche with no real ambition to join the popular kids. That didn't sit well with her so she decided it was time to act. One day, out of the blue, she tossed me the high school class directory.

"See this list?" her tone was sharp.

I froze. I could only imagine what she had planned.

"YOU are going to call every popular girl in this directory and

80

make plans to go on a play date," she announced.

At first I laughed. I thought she was joking, but she was not. Now I was in high school, mind you. Play date? Hell, a rogue zit could take you down the popularity list in a heartbeat. I was pretty, but slightly overweight, had skin problems (once Sherri Smith asked if I had measles during a facial acne outbreak), and definitely my puberty-infested body was no match for the almost-*Playboy* bunny. It had been made clear to me all of my life, as if it weren't obvious by looking at her, that Janet had always been one of the most popular girls in her high school. How could it be that her daughter was not following in those footsteps? I knew her legacy, but could never quite become one of the chosen girls. That was one of her qualities, not mine, although she often blurred the two.

It isn't as if I didn't try. I was a cheerleader for my freshman season, but that didn't quite measure up. Private school cheerleaders are not like the competitive super-doll public school variety. They were precise, hotbox, flawless machines, ready to jump at the sight of a ball...well, you know what I mean. Anyway, unlike a public school squad, my private school stressed academics over appearance, and their cheerleaders really didn't have that same "t and a" factor. We didn't have the hunger of our public school counterparts. When the basketball team is just as celebrated as the Optimist's Club, it's hardly a time to cheer.

Take our "hello cheer," usually most bright and shiny cheerleaders, like my mother was many years ago, elaborately executed their greeting to the other team in a way that rivaled Souza's marching band. Our "hello cheer" was just that...we walked out to the guest team, stood in a line, raised our right arms and said, "Hello," with a lame pom-pom arm gesture and pathetic jump. Then we turned around and went back to our seats.

I soon realized Mom was still looking at me, serious about this play date idea of hers. "Mom, I am not friends with most of those girls. You can't ask me to do this." I was sick to my stomach. This could be the final stake in my sad popularity coffin.

"I'm sick of you not being popular. YOU are going to call the most popular girls you know and just ask them to include you." Her face was determined and war-like. I knew this was not just a suggestion. "And one play date is going to do that?" I was in agony, face fuming.

"It's a start. Now start calling or else!" She gave me that crazed look and clenched her teeth, raising her fist in the air. I was absolutely horrified. It was my worst nightmare, calling classmates who, if they weren't making fun of me, were definitely not interested in doing anything with me. I'd rather chew off my own arm.

Janet stood over me. "Start!" She pointed her red-nailed finger at the rotary phone on Dad's side of the bed.

"I can't do this with you over my shoulder." I was getting panicky, desperate to think of a way out.

"You better do this." She got in my face. Her horse whisper was even more terrifying than her yelling. Dad was in bed, resting, ignoring us. He'd had a hard week and apparently didn't want to risk getting either of us more agitated.

Eyes tearing, I picked up the receiver. She glared and left the room with a loud slam of the door. I looked at the list through my waterworks. I saw my dad, somehow totally asleep. Although he hadn't stopped her, his presence gave me the strength to get through the first call. It was Stacy Abner, a slim, athletic jock that kind of said "hi" in the halls, who has probably been flirting with boys since daycare. I thought maybe I had an outside chance with her.

"Uh, is Stacy there?" My voice was shaking. I almost dropped the heavy, putty-colored receiver.

"Yes, who may I ask is calling?" asked a pleasant voice.

"It's Leanna," I said.

"Who," inquired the lady?

"I go to school with Stacy." I cleared my throat.

"Oh, okay. One moment."

An eternity passed. I was sweating and shaking.

"Hey. Who is this?" Stacey got on the line, her voice tough.

"Leanna," I announced.

"Who?" she sneered.

"Leanna. We're in gym class together, Ms. White's—" I started.

"Oh…yeah, what's up," she interrupted.

"I was wondering if you wanted to go to see the Boston Pops at Pine Knob," I asked.

Silence. I almost hung up.

"Uh, is this a party you're inviting me to?" Her voice was hateful.

"No, an outing." Idiot, I thought.

"Oh. Well, I'm busy," she nastily replied.

"Okay. Good enough for me. Bye!" Relieved, I hung up the phone.

"What happened?" Janet had been listening from the hall all along.

"She was sick," I lied.

"Dial again, goddamit ." Her voice low.

I was trying to figure out who would bring the least damage to my now-very-frail ego. Still feeling queasy, I dialed Gail Baynor. Gail was yuppier than most yuppies with Levi's cords, a sports shirt as her permanent uniform, long hair, and preppy docks, even on the tennis court. Gail wasn't stuck up, but definitely in a different world, a different caliber. Oil and water was more cohesive than the two of us.

"Hi Mrs. Baynor, this is Leanna." I got a bit more momentum. I felt like I was selling Green Stamps or maybe a timeshare.

She was actually a nice lady; I could practically hear her facelift shift over the phone.

"Oh…Leanna?" she asked.

"Yes." Good sign, I thought. She sounded pleasant, or was I just being hopeful?

"Anything wrong?" her voice went a bit panicky. There were some stories of Gail using her smarts to intimidate some of the students. That's one thing going for her.

"No, I was wondering if Gail was there," I said.

"Yes. Hold on." I heard the phone hit the wall.

A few minutes later, a very expressive voice says: "Yes?"

"Hey, Gail. It's Leanna." I could practically hear her wheels turning.

"Uh…Hi." I just knew that *what in world are you doing calling me* was rolling around in that blonde head of hers.

"Yeah…Hi." I suddenly wanted to hang up.

Silence.

"Um, well my mom was wondering—I mean, I was wondering what you were doing this Saturday?"

"Well, something, I'm sure," she replied. Smart ass.

"Uh, okay," I said, ready to bid my farewell.

"Why?" she prompted, probably hoping for a good story for tomorrow's English class.

"Well, did you want to go see the Boston Pops at Pine Knob?"

"Boston Pops?"

"Yeah, it's a symphony and…" This was a mistake.

"I know what it is." She laughed.

"Okay. Great." Maybe she'll…

"No thanks. Gotta run," she exclaimed.

"Oh, okay. Thanks." Defeated, I hung up the phone. What a bitch. Janet was not in the hallway. She must have gotten distracted or else she'd be here, terrorizing me. I made a few more calls with responses like, "Didn't you already graduate?" or "Which class are you in?" And the best one: "Hell no, zit face!" This was getting somewhat demeaning. I got down to the "N's"…and finally I hit pay dirt.

"Hello." It was the voice of Sue Nine.

"Hi, Mrs. Nine," I was happy to hear a kind voice.

"Hello…" She trailed off.

"It's Leanna," I said.

"Oh, hi Leanna!" she sounded genuinely happy to hear me. Either that or she was a good actress. I loved Mrs. and Mr. Nine. They were both friendly and eternally positive people with a family law practice. I liked Diane, who was a volleyball jock and popular kid in school, perky and smart. She was certainly more popular than me, but wasn't arrogant about it. Finally, this could be it.

"Can I speak with Diane?"

"Sure. How are you?"

"Oh, very good, Mrs. Nine," I responded, slightly taken aback. I was so used to being brushed off I barely knew how to react when someone was being nice.

"Great. Say hi to your mom and dad." My father had started "The

Dad's Club" with Mr. Nine who was an awesome help to Dad.

"Hello?" I heard Diane's cheery voice over the phone.

"Diane?" I was crossing my fingers.

"Hi."

"Hey, I'm wondering if you wanted to do something Saturday." I popped the question.

"Sure," she said without hesitation.

"Really?" I was elated.

"Yeah."

"Cool!" I was so relieved. If Diane Nine wasn't popular enough for Janet, I was staying in a Ho-Jo's and getting a lawyer tonight. Maybe Mr. Nine could take my case.

"Boston Pops is playing at Pine Knob," I informed her.

"I know!" she exclaimed.

"Wanna go?"

"Yes!" And the rest is history; I had moved higher up on the popularity food chain based on some creative math. There was certainly some subtraction from the rejections I got, but I think that "yes" definitely redeemed me. Janet calmed down. Diane and I definitely clicked (and some forty years later, she became the literary agent for this book).

I was certainly grateful that she lent me some of her popularity by association and in turn I was able to leverage that to become quite well-liked in my own right. It's a tricky game, that high school pecking order. For me it was made much more precarious because of the pressure from Janet. I realize that she had good intentions, but her follow through could have used some finesse. That play date plan might have easily backfired had it not for been the one "yes" that I received.

Somehow things have a way of working out in Janet's favor. She's had a charmed life. Always has. It's great material for a book, but hell on my self-esteem.

# Chapter 14: Queen for a Day

*Work your glitter girls, the brighter the bling
the more his wallet will sing!*

Sweet sixteen is a tender and pivotal time in a young girl's life and most parents do everything they can to make it memorable. Janet wanted the same for her daughter.

It was the night before my birthday, which happened to be on a Saturday in 1978. It was the time of "Funkytown," Parliament Funkadelic, sex symbol Peter Frampton making his guitar talk, Electric Light Orchestra faking a concert, Queen gender-bending rock and roll, and The Rolling Stones taking a misguided detour into disco music.

It was, in my opinion, from the army tank style of cars to the faded bell-bottoms, lace flowing tops, and black lighted Bee Gees posters, the best time to be alive. If you had a problem with a boy or had a bully on your ass, there were no damning impacts from social media and cyberspace...and "sexting" was limited to 8-track tapes played in smoky rooms for the disenfranchised.

Vietnam was finally over and President Jimmy Carter, to the disappointment of my Republican parents, had just been elected a year before. I got the news in typing class when Cara Johnson (her dad was a judge) came in with a big green and white "CARTER for President" button. Buttons were popular back then as both a fashion statement and way to support a cause, sort of like wearing a Facebook post or a Tweet on your chest. The class booed when they read her shiny metal message. Republicans train their kids at a young age...usually at

86

parties, non-altruistic field trips, and even peace rallies.

In fact, I was social chairman of the Young Republicans Club whose sole job, oddly enough, was to secure liquor for all mixers and social events. And, of course, it was good social training, which pleased Janet to no end. My best mate, Amy, and I threw the best campaign parties with as much creativity as Elton John put into making "The Yellow Album." Ok, not a direct analogy, but it was indeed a special time. I started paying more attention to my parents' parties in my teen years. From the time I was just a pup, when I heard the murmur and steady hum of guests downstairs, I knew my parents were happy and everything was going to be all right. I didn't even have a drink; I just liked the "happy" vibe of parties. It was contagious.

However, beyond the party walls, other events loomed large. The "energy crisis" was building and the Iran hostages were on the front pages. But still in our little section of the world, it seemed like everyone was aware of those things, but didn't want them to interfere with their fun. It was one nation under a groove, getting down "just for the funk of it." Of course this free-spirited atmosphere was perfect for Janet. Her antics fit in nicely with the easy-going, carefree attitude. And being in Detroit, music and partying was a big part of our lives, especially mine.

Janet approached me before my big day. "I want you to have the most special sweet sixteen in the world. And I'm not talking boring cake, ice cream and a movie." She said it matter-of-factly, like I hadn't been living with her for the past fifteen years, eleven months, and twenty-something days.

"Sounds good, Mom. We could take all my friends out to eat." I suggested with a smile.

"But where do we party after that?" Janet threw up her hands.

"Good point," I said, thinking down the road that college life certainly shouldn't be a problem.

"If you want that special night to be in a stuffy restaurant, it's up to you," she said, obviously with ulterior motives.

"No way!" I liked the idea of something special. "We could just invite everyone over here," I reasoned. I'd grown up seeing the amazing parties my parents could throw with just a moment's notice.

"Oh, I'm sick of handling the cleanup. We need to outsource," Janet declared. "It's all about outsourcing these days."

Actually, I remember quite well the "clean up" of Janet's parties. Flashback to my eighth birthday: Janet had a group of her theatre friends over and I had awoken from a nap. I went downstairs. People were lying on the floor, passed out all over, cigarettes and drinks littered the carpet. I heard a moan come from the bathroom and echo through the checkered black-and-white tile hallway. My mother, face down, was vomiting an odd cranberry-colored substance all over her beautiful silver gown, hair still up in a chignon. I immediately grabbed her by the shoulders and turned her on her side. She gasped for air, vomited more, and then breathed normally before passing out. I cleaned the mess, including Janet. I couldn't lift her, but made sure she was upright and able to breathe. If only that cleaning guy from my birth had made house calls.

I snapped out of my flashback when Janet started putting a headband on me.

"Mom!" I exclaimed, adjusting the rather tight gold velour fashion statement.

"Hold still! You've got to do something with that hair. Anyway, I know you'll love this. Wear your gold dress. Everyone in 'the Woods' is in." Janet reported.

"Wow, that's going to be great." I loved our neighbors. Brianna, Rebecca, Bernie, John Ormon (the Mayor of Huntington Woods), Doug, Karen (from the Hot Dog Lunch!), and her mom, Lisa (harpist for the Detroit Symphony) were great friends. We were like a well-heeled gang, spending every holiday together until I was twenty-five.

Once I was meticulously dressed in my Sweet sixteen getup, Dad called upstairs. "Leanna, honey, I'll be in the car."

Dad looked smart in his tailored shirt, vest, and slacks. Now fifty-six, he was aging gracefully and still as handsome as the day Mom met him. He seemed excited to go out. He loved to party with Janet, which was what I'd heard they did a lot of before I was born. While he had been absent much of my early childhood, by the time I left grade school he had more time to be with me, and we developed a very strong bond. If we weren't watching *Star Trek*, we were discussing "white noise" or articles in *Scientific American* about The Red Shift. (It was some philosophical debate about life's origins or our existence. Very '70s.)

"Dad!" I shouted out the door. "Where are we going?"

"To Flint, to a transvestite bar!" he answered matter-of-factly.

"WHAT?" I couldn't believe it. I guess they did party at Woodstock.

Mom shouted from upstairs, as usual she was still applying her makeup when everyone was fully dressed, "It's the only place that serves minors. And they have a dance floor. Perfect!" Well, so much for stuffy Republicans.

Their theater group, the Royal Oak Civic Theater, was a weekly social and creative outlet for the young couple. With television limited to three channels in those days, theater was a fantastic way to occupy your leisure time and inspire creativity. These thespians were talented residents, mainly in their twenties and thirties, not planning to leave for New York or LA, but sincerely gifted writers, directors and actors who were just as serious about "their art" as they were about throwing a good party or hitting all the dance clubs before closing. They produced musicals and plays of the day: *Dark At The Top of The Stairs*, *You Can't Take It With You*, and *Philadelphia Story* to name a few, as well as putting on some originals. And it wasn't just Mom who had all the fun. Dad acted and sang in many of them.

He shined as Colonel Pickering in *My Fair Lady* (or *Pygmalion*) and below he is (last one, left) with the cast of *Dark At The Top of The Stairs*. As a young child watching their shows, I was mesmerized by both of my parents. Below, they both are featured in the *Royal Oak Daily Tribune*, May, 1959. Dad is in the middle of the picture under the heading "Comedy In The Making" as C.K. Dexter Haven, a lead in *The Philadelphia Story* (Cary Grant played his role in the 1940 movie) and Mom is making up the leading lady beneath the article on Dad. There were also mentions for other notorious members of the group, such as my Uncle Fred (who wrote plays for both Janet and Bill), his wife Aunt Hazel, and their two children Debbie and Denise who were fast family friends along with Aunt Fee Fee and the gay blade…and Janet's naughty partner in crime… Uncle Chester. (You'll see him cavorting with our little star in a few photos, he's in the corner lower left next to Janet.)

In fact, these artists were proudly liberal and discernibly open-minded. They had indeed exposed my parents to people from all walks of life far away from the social norms of the Kentucky hills. For example, it was a sad day when our good friends Nick and Sam broke up. Sam dumped Nick and had the nerve to get married...to a woman! Blasphemy! I was devastated. Besides, they had a kickin' pool and ranch house.

So, finally, the entire Woods gang showed up and we all caravanned out to my first adult "bar experience" in Flint, Michigan.

Flint is a town about an hour away from the Detroit suburbs, mainly working-class families, which made me wonder why in the world were cross-dressers thinking having a bar here? (Now it's known for that terrible lead-in-the-water scandal, but we knew even back then the area had troubles.) No doubt some law or statue made serving minors possible (which might have been a good idea since the water was atrocious even then) or maybe the small bar had just gone unnoticed. But there we were at 8:00 p.m., in the relative quiet August night with an unmistakable "boom, boom, boom" of the disco beat coming from the far corner of the dimly lit street. Oddly enough, my friends' parents seemed totally comfortable, and I mean even the Mayor of Huntington Woods. My friends, on the other hand, seemed a bit more...stunned.

Flash. Flash. Flash! I blinked and what appeared to be Jean Harlow greeted me.

"Hello, darling!" She motioned us to come in with her long nails and sparkling boa.

*Mom's long lost sister?* I thought.

"Welcome. We hear it's a very special night for you! I'm Miss Divine," said the buxom blonde with even more makeup than Janet had ever attempted.

"Hi," I said meekly. We made our way through the strobe lights, false eyelashes, and electric eye shadow.

"Here's your table." She waved her long, thick-gloved arm and pointed to an adorable corner setup. And sure enough the girls—as I decided to call them—had gone out of their way to prepare for my entire party.

The slick soda-shop-style round booth was adorable, cake with my name on it, plates, and party favors flooded the table. And what décor! *Who's their planner? Could use them for my wedding one day,* I thought.

"Darling!" Another diva rushed at me from the direction of the spotted strobe light.

"Hey, girl—oh, it's you, Mom," I said, confusing her with the "talent."

"What do you think?" She smiled, proudly.

"Amazing." And it truly was. "Really sweet, Mom." I had to give it to her. Who would have a dance floor and cocktails for underage youth complete with glamorous girls in flowing gowns? All with flawless makeup? Janet, that's who.

"I want you to meet Ruby." Right behind Janet was the main house diva. Yes, Ruby was a six foot five vision in red spandex and spangles with a bright sparkle dress, pointy breasts, and matching boots with the parliament heels, pancake makeup, and a beauty queen hairdo to rival even the goddess of fire, Pele. Large fake lashes, perfectly lined red lips, drooping diamond earrings, and matching bracelet and necklace completed the shiny ensemble. She was ready for the Royal Opera, or an alternative bar in Flint, Michigan.

With a surprisingly strong grasp, she whisked me onto the dance floor, with Janet gleefully in tow. Wondering what to do next, I looked at my friends eagerly sipping forbidden drinking and tearing into my cake.

I felt a tap on my shoulder and turned to face another extremely tall, heavily made-up lady who said in a high-pitched tone, "I'd like the honor of this dance!"

Wait, was I leading? What's going on here! I froze. They were playing the twelve inch version of the hit single "Funkytown."

Ruby put her big, manicured hands on my waist, stealing me back. "Won't you take me to...Funkytown?" she crooned.

"Now, give Ruby a sweet sixteen kiss!" Janet pulled us closer together. I searched the floor for my dad. He was in back playing pool with the mayor. The diva puckered up, getting closer and closer to my lips.

"Mom!" I shouted. She howled with laughter. I turned my cheek just in time to get a cheek imprint Salvador Dali would have envied.

"Happy sweet sixteen, darling!" exclaimed Ruby, who seemed genuinely moved to be hosting my birthday. Then all the girls started waving their boas. "Happy Sweet Sixteen!" they shouted.

Then the beat changed. It was that familiar warm up to one of the most popular dances around. "Ooooooooooh, ooh, ooh, ooh, ooh, oooooooh....*do it* (whispered)..." It was that unmistakable opening refrain.

Thank goodness for "The Hustle." I broke out and started dancing like my life depended on it. Of course my friends and I always practiced the latest dances whenever we could. So I was in my element. At that moment I decided to take a page from Janet's book and just let loose. I mean, if I couldn't do it in this accepting atmosphere, where could I?

At first Janet seemed taken aback, but soon she smiled her acknowledgement as she watched me shake my groove thing.

"Yeah, baby. Let's do it." I said, striking a *Saturday Night Fever* pose, disco ball whirling above.

"OOOOOOOOOH, oooh oooh ooh ooooooh! *Do It!*" My entire group of friends popped out of the booth and onto the dance floor joining me and my new pals, Ruby, Miss Devine, and the other glamour girls. We did the entire song perfectly, with a finish that rivaled John Travolta in the movie finale.

Maybe there were still things I could learn from my mom, and even Miss Divine. I just couldn't tell Janet that. I'd never hear the end of it.

# Chapter 15: The Flying Trapeze

*Seal the deal with a diamond and you're done!*

Soon I was off to college in Ann Arbor, leaving Bill and Janet back where they started, as a popular social couple enjoying all that suburban life had to offer. One year after graduating from The University of Michigan, at twenty-two, I moved to Chicago and attended improv classes at the infamous Second City Theater, home to movie stars and *Saturday Night Live* alums like Mike Meyers and Tina Fey as well as the late Chris Farley (who was in some of my classes along with Tim Meadows and Joel Murray). I had "made it" to level three in the Second City class scheme, so faith in my abilities was at a high. That summer I made a trip home to visit my parents and I was practically bursting with the good vibes of my progress. Huntington Woods remained largely unchanged. Its nicely trimmed, tree-lined streets and inviting upper-middle-class brick homes untouched by the economic demise of the city of Detroit, only three miles away. The protective bubble of that comedic world was no match for the sobering realities of suburbia. No matter how confident I became in my abilities, coming back home always had a way of reminding me of my identity struggles as a kid. Fortunately, this time there was a distraction thanks to the Johnsons.

My dear family friends, Bob and Arlene Johnson, were your typical Midwestern couple with an overcrowded garage and a house next to a major freeway. Arlene wore a Ralph Lauren cotton dresses, while Bob wore golf shirts, khakis, and Top-Siders. Their topics of conversation typically included aging parents, new grandchildren and

Arlene's new crush, *Dirty Dancing*'s Patrick Swayze.

"Bob, why can't you dance like Patrick Swayze?"

"Who says I can't?" Bob grabbed Arlene and started the two-step in the middle of the kitchen while "Wheel of Fortune" blared on the TV.

Their life was a never-ending cycle of normal. Bob, an insurance salesman, had just retired, so they decided it was time to splurge on the trendy new retiree dream of that generation. They purchased the latest model Winnebago, and they had invited us to accompany them on its virgin cruise.

That Wednesday while getting ready to visit the couple, Janet was in a tizzy over the eternal question: "What to wear?"

"Just go ahead and get in the car! I'll be right there." She swished a black Chanel purse around her hip and checked her silhouette in one of the many full-length mirrors throughout the house. We were late, as usual. Dad and I had already waited for hours while Janet changed into, out of, and back into her trademark Anne Klein black cat suit. Last year her favorite was a neon pink number which she wore at Christmas Mass, sans bra. Years past, Janet again made an impression with her white Vittadini backless one-piece palazzo pants suit and, you guessed it, no bra to finish the look.

I stared out the window from the back seat of our Lincoln Town Car. Ford was my dad's biggest client at the time. When he called on GM, he rented a Cadillac, of course. He has always been a skilled businessman. It was a good thing Dad was an auto executive. Janet went on to have a history of crashing a few Caddies.

Although we were expecting it, Janet's sudden appearance startled us. With a flash of black and blonde, and a whiff of Chanel No. 5, she crash-landed in the front passenger's seat, purse and red nails flailing. "Let's go, dammit!" she yelped, like we'd been the ones holding her up all morning. Janet lit a cigarette, puffed once, and then blew smoke toward the closed window. Dad gave her a bit of a smirk, and we zoomed off to Sterling Heights and Janet's worst nightmare, working-class suburbia.

Bob and Arlene adored Janet. She epitomized a type of extroversion they never could quite comprehend, but they had fun with her and really liked the fact she was so different from everyone else they knew. Janet, Dad, Bob, and Arlene had developed a great friendship from the day they all met each other at the Rigid Tool Convention in Boise, Idaho.

Bob and Arlene were also a real departure from my parents' usual auto executive crowd, but especially from their "theatre" friends who partied like rock stars and performed in a play every now and again. Surely Uncle Chester and Aunt Fee Fee could have transformed Bob and Arlene's Winnebago into a 1960's "love van" complete with *Barbarella*-style shag carpeted ceilings and smoky round portal windows that made the hippies blush with the shenanigans going on inside. Needless to say, my parents enjoyed a diverse social circle.

Dad finally delivered us safely in the Town Car, easing skillfully into the Johnson's driveway. The happy couple greeted us immediately. They couldn't wait to show off their brand-new Winnebago, with its brown siding, green gingham curtains, and the classic protrusion over the driver's seat that denoted a built-in bed.

At first, Janet was cautious and inched her way up to the boxy vehicle, a bit unnerved by how average it was. When she saw it was safe, she boomed out, "Impressive! Very avant-garde!" She then pointed to the rear. "What's that on the back?"

"Bicycles," Arlene answered.

"Smashing! What taste!" Janet put a hand on her hip and nodded with approval.

Bob smiled and handed her a Budweiser (other than Martinis her favorite vintage), excited to have received Janet's fashionista blessing on their new purchase. For all her preoccupation with wealth, power, and social graces, Janet was still that party girl from Kentucky who could drink anybody under the table including frat boys, bikers, sailors, and even the seasoned auto executives, all while discussing the latest stars and gossip: *LA Law*'s Harry Hamlin, John-John Kennedy, Baby 'M' (the first surrogate baby), Farrah Fawcett in *The Burning Bed,* and lesbians.

Dad and Bob began checking the tire pressure and packing the

Winnebago with the additional drinks and snacks we'd brought. I happened to be the only young adult going on the trip and as I watched the retirement-age adults milling about the six-wheeled monolith in the driveway, I began to wonder, *Is this it? My future? Joy rides in a mobile home? Does it all just come down to transportation?*

At last, everything was ready to go, and we settled into our chosen seats. Dad and Bob, of course, were up front. Janet sat right behind them and Arlene and I faced off on the side couches.

We rolled out of the driveway and, to my pleasant surprise, Bob and Arlene's new motorhome was in motion, cruising easily down the side streets like a compact car. We sat high above the station wagons and Ford Fiestas parked along the sidewalks. After passing row upon row of cookie-cutter driveways with their matching campers, we eventually met the highway to Sarnia. The route led up the coast of Lake Huron and headed toward the thumb of Michigan. The state has always been called "the big mitten," an imaginative term made up by the natives who at the very least got to check out the state on a map. Michiganians even point to a spot on their hands to indicate where they're going. (I think the pointing thing is in their DNA.)

Janet started chatting with Arlene right away about the new outfit she had bought me for a job interview. "I have no doubt it will get her a job and a promotion. Dress for success, I say—and knockers up!" Janet exclaimed with a leg kick.

I remember that dress quite vividly. It was skintight, and I'm surprised I could bend over to pull my resume out of my briefcase. Despite Janet's confidence (in the dress), I didn't get that job, but I did get the phone numbers of five guys in the office. I thought Janet would be upset, but the opposite was true. "Bravo! Now seal the deal with a diamond and you're done!" she sang, raising her Budweiser.

That summer, after improv training at Second City, I had been thinking, against Dad's better judgment, about embarking on a standup comedy career full time. Janet loved the idea because it was her chance to finally become famous (by default) and maybe even have her picture on the cover of *The New York Times* fashion section. My success could redeem her fateful mistake of not taking the position with Revlon.

Now she was banking on me living "the dream" so she could manage my career (which wasn't such a far-fetched idea) like *Auntie Mame* or Brooke Shields' mother.

After two hours' worth of RV partying and a quick stop at a restaurant in Lake St. Clare for a late lunch, Bob turned the big camper toward home. As we drove along, the landscape of trees and sky meshed into one long, hypnotic brushstroke. As we were about to merge onto the entrance ramp for I-94 South, Michigan did, to paraphrase Simon and Garfunkel, "seem like a dream."

Janet impulsively unbuckled her seatbelt, stood up, holding her cigarette and ashtray tightly, and staggered towards the back of the Winnebago. We all knew where she was headed, right toward the fridge. Just then, Bob turned and accelerated onto the highway as Janet was grabbing for the Budweiser. The motion from the quick turn propelled her across the motorhome into Arlene's seat. She then ricocheted into the opposite side and hit the door squarely with a slam. The force busted the lock and the door flew wide open: launching our style princess out of the Winnebago—cat suit, Bud, and all—into the path of four lanes of merging traffic. Arlene screamed. My mouth dropped open. Bob hit the brakes and at the same moment Dad jumped out of the Winnebago to prevent what could possibly have been the greatest tragedy of my life.

Paralyzed with fear, I sat, waiting for the worst. Strange thoughts kept running through my head. Headlines: "Detroit Celeb Model Morphs into Black Designer Pancake," "How I Lost My Life, But Not My Bud" in *Women's Wear Daily* or WABC-TV anchors on the scene: "Today we have an RV fatality. I'm Bill Bonds here with the designer scoop."

When I could move again, I braced myself for the horror and looked out. Janet lay on the shoulder of the road, dusty and shaken. Dad stood over her for a moment and then sat down beside her to hold her hand while her other one was still clutching the Budweiser. Hardly missing a beat, Janet sat up, raised her bottle in the air, and said, "This Bud's for you!" The crowd of onlookers started applauding.

"Is she with the circus?" I overheard one cop ask, and not the first time I'd heard that question, I might add.

Later, we discovered, to our amazement, she'd had the wherewithal to roll away from traffic just in the nick of time. It was as if her Vittadini ensemble had empowered her with cat-like reflexes. The wheels of the Winnebago—wheels that surely would have crushed her a few moments before—now protected her as they blocked the roadway. More and more motorists crawled past the scene, rubbernecking and probably hoping for gore. What they saw instead was a pretty, well-dressed woman chatting with the police and waving to the passersby as if it was an outdoor social mixer.

Janet escaped totally unscathed from her near-death experience. And she didn't hesitate to tell the Highway Patrol Chief he needed a bit more color and a better quality fabric for his uniforms. "And for God's sake, Willie," she said with a wink, "cut out the crullers and jellies."

After finishing with the police, we buckled Janet in her seat, with a six-pack directly within reach—for safety precautions, of course. In less than a minute, Janet was smoking, toasting her survival, and joking, reveling in her familiar place as the center of attention.

Finally, we were on the road again. Dad and Bob decided to sue the motor home company for the faulty door and split the profits. Arlene sat in shock, as stiff as a board, all the way back to suburbia. Janet seemed oblivious and continued to recount the details of her most recent misadventure as if we hadn't been there to witness it.

Exhausted from the trauma, I slid down into the cushy sofa, realizing that for better or worse, nothing she did truly surprised me anymore. These many years later, I'm still trying to grasp how raw and devastating the Winnebago incident could have been.

At the time, for me, it was just another chapter in the life of The Daily Janet.

# Chapter 16: Lights Out

*Nothing livens up an afternoon like a good tragedy!*

After my stint at Second City, I moved to New York in 1988 to hone my craft and tackle the standup comedy stage in my mid-twenties. Thrilled by my non-practical dream of "showbiz," Janet was, of course, a frequent visitor to my Upper West Side apartment and loved to watch me perform at Stand Up New York, the Gotham Comedy Club, or any place where I could get a booking (including sushi restaurants, hot dog stands and old folks homes). Sometimes when I looked at her from the stage, I could almost imagine her thoughts: *My little girl might be more like me than she realizes. Now, if she would only wear lip liner and show her cleavage, she'd be perfect.*

Janet picked the "perfect" time to arrive in NYC. What New Yorkers had feared since 1972 finally happened—we had a real live blackout in the summer of 2003. Although its impact paled in comparison to other major tragedies such as 9/11, the blackout was definitely a huge scare. Power was knocked out along the entire East Coast for three days and it was challenging to get around New York at night, with no illumination at all, no neon signs, streets lights, or theater marquees to light the way.

On the bright side, it also turned out to be an opportune time for my Latino neighbors to party in the streets, dancing as their boom boxes blared nearby. Who would have known "blackout" in Spanish meant block party? I must say the dancing and festivities helped keep morale high as the crowds rushed to the stores for bread, milk, water and batteries. It made the blackout one of the more pleasant catastrophes I've ever experienced.

About an hour before she was supposed to arrive, Janet called me from the George Washington Bridge to say she was on her way. When the hour passed and no Janet had landed, I became worried. I called her cell number over and over with no luck. When I finally got through, she told me she had gotten lost. Only when she began to give details of her adventure did I realize how worried I should have been. Driving her new Mercedes, she had ended up taking a "detour" to the Upper West Side—upper to the tune of Malcolm X Boulevard.

"Mom, where are you?" I figured she would name a gas station or some bodega.

"I stopped at this charming, rundown parking lot when I saw a nice group of men standing around a burning can," she answered, quite matter-of-factly. All I could think of was the scene in *Bonfire of the Vanities* where Sherman (or Tom Hanks if you saw the movie) can't get back on the highway because trash cans are blocking the way. Mayhem ensues.

"You went up to a group of guys standing in a parking lot around a burning trashcan?" I sat down on the bed and stared at the wall. Visions of Janet, a Gloria Vanderbilt version of Joan of Arc, warming her hands over the burning can talking Gucci and celebrity gossip while the men combed through her purse and sped off in her car. Apparently, too stunned to even consider a robbery, the guys were in awe of the rich, lost white lady who had the nerve to approach them for directions in the first place. In the end, she told me that they had exchanged phone numbers.

"Now, Leroy, call me, darling. And leave that no-good bitch! I don't trust her either!" She waved to them all, did her quick traditional leg kick in the air, jumped into the car and sped off into the inner city landscape in a cloud of NYC road dust.

Janet arrived at my apartment hours later, excited that she had met some new friends. The fact that she pulled the Mercedes-Benz up over the curb almost to the door of my apartment building, right in front of the security guard, was an indication she was ready to party.

Janet sprang out of the car to confront the security guard who scolded her with a "Lady, you can't park here!"

"Oh I've driven fifteen hours and I'm exhausted! You wouldn't happen to have a little nip, would you?"

Janet buzzed my intercom, and I anxiously ran downstairs to greet her. Acting as if nothing out of the ordinary had happened that day, she motioned for me to grab her bags. I gave the car the once-over and was relieved to see it had miraculously kept its hubcaps. After schlepping all the bags upstairs, I came back down and spent the next twenty minutes trying to find a parking spot while Janet was chatting up Hank, our doorman. I finally settled on a nearby garage.

"Hank, you have to come with us to the 21 Club." She was already making big plans. "I can't wait to rub elbows with the stars!"

I had a feeling it was going to be a long night. The very moment we got to the elevator, the button had quit working and the lobby lights clicked off. All we could see was the faint glow of the emergency sign. Stunned, we turned around and walked with several others out of the lobby and into the street. Masses of people were spilling out of the buildings. What was going on? The neighbors had congregated on the sidewalks to drink, play dominos, and gab. Soon everyone was dancing in the streets.

As Janet gleefully told Hank about how her new friend Jamal had said she was a real "sexy, white girl," I began to imagine a number of conspiracy theories and alien conquest scenarios that could overtake us at any minute. My heart sank. I should have taken my emergency 9-1-1 "to go" bag more seriously. From what I remember, all I had in it was water, tampons, and Chap Stick. Janet, however, was ecstatic. "I love New York!" she yelled out loud over the salsa to no one in particular, shaking her hips and drinking the *Cervesa* offered to her by a young Latino man. They started dancing the Merengue on the sidewalk.

"Oooooh, Enrique, you are a natural, darling."

The sun was setting. The food in the refrigerator would spoil soon. And all Janet could think about was grinding with the locals. With a sudden and unexpected look of concern, Janet's voice rang out, "Wait, we forgot the essentials!"

I thought the essentials, at least for our current situation, were batteries and canned goods. I immediately found out that Janet was more concerned with beer, wine, cigarettes, and Anacin. The small bodega (or convenience store) was packed. Everyone scurried for whatever was left on the shelves. I raced for bottled water and batteries for my flashlight. Janet, having disappeared into the crowd for ten minutes, approached me from the other side of the store with a six-pack of Budweiser and a look of utter defeat.

"We didn't make it on time," Janet exclaimed, pointing to the darkened store fridge, minus its usual buzz of electricity. "The beer isn't cold, and they're out of Kools."

She then handed me a couple of vigil candles gilded with an image of the Virgin Mary and an array of frozen dinners.

"Janet, we can't eat these," I protested.

"Don't lecture me now. This is an emergency!"

I just shook my head and put them on the non-working conveyor belt as the cashier laughed and said something incomprehensible. I only know it was Spanish, and heard *loca* and *gringa* as she manually calculated our cost and took the last bit of my cash. Hauling our bags of apocalypse foodstuffs, we actually had to push our way through the crowds all the way down the street and back up the stairs to my apartment.

"Oh, tragedy is so exciting," Janet said as she walked into my studio apartment and gazed out the panoramic window. While she was enjoying the sunset and chaos, I started working on our disaster plan and tried to remember anyone I knew who owned their own water supply or maybe a farm with livestock. A few moments later, a knock on the door startled us. To Janet's delight, on the other side were five New York City firemen, all somewhere in their mid-thirties. These calendar-ready studs were going door-to-door to make sure everyone was all right: a dream come true for Janet and most women.

"Oh, hello, boys. I didn't know you made house calls." Janet struck a vamp pose. "Come on in and have a beer. New York is so much fun!"

"Hello, ma'am," said the fireman "We have to evacuate the building."

"Great Scots! I just brought my bags up here."

"A leak in the water main is causing a problem with the foundation," he continued. "It seems the leak, in combination with the construction next door, may cause the building to collapse. You will need to leave this apartment in twenty minutes."

"Why?" Janet pondered. "There can't be a water leak. I was just in Harlem and everyone was fine."

"I'm sorry, ma'am. But you have to go," piped up another hot fireman.

"Oh, nonsense, boys, there's always time for a nightcap." She smiled, ran to the kitchen counter and got her six-pack. Within seconds, she was distributing bottles. The men laughed and starting drinking. And poof! Like magic, we had an instant hot-guy hall party.

"Let's take this shindig downstairs, boys!" Janet grabbed her gold Armani clutch and left me standing in the doorway as she sauntered off with five guys, drinking and laughing. "Pop down as soon as you can, dear. I'll save you a *Cervasa* and a dance with Enrique. And bring all my bags with you!"

With the firemen totally captivated by Janet's charms and vice-versa, I got busy with the evacuation process—this time sorting what we absolutely needed from what we might end up sacrificing to the potential collapse. With only twenty minutes to think and to pack, the only thing of Janet's I was completely sure of was her medication. God knows she needed her pills: Valium, hydrocodone, Cymbalta, cholesterol medicine, low-grade Valium, Provigil, Nuvigil, and that was just the shortlist. I also remembered some incidental items, passports and money as well as the basics we would need for a hotel stay, a couple of pairs of panties and our toothbrushes.

Everyone in the building had gathered at the corner of Columbus Avenue and 97th Street. When I arrived downstairs panting, there was Janet, in all her glory, a fireman on each arm and others gathered around her. Paying no mind to the catastrophe that might ensue, she was already on a first-name basis with all of them. I heard her ask if they knew Jamal and Leroy from the parking lot campfire.

"Kevin," she asked one blonde, well-built lieutenant, "is it legal to burn a fire in a can in New York?"

While I focused on the details (whether to take a pair of panties or all of them) and a few more serious things (whether or not I would ever see my apartment again), Janet had escaped death, not once but two times in one evening. She had then turned her life-threatening experiences into a flirtatious party complete with dancing, music, booze, and hot six-foot-tall guys. She was clearly working the New York sidewalk post-disaster.

And that's how I got a photograph of Mom with eight NYFD hunks. According to Janet, *la dolce vita* can be anywhere you decide it is, even on the streets of New York during a blackout.

*Photo credit: Geraldine Salvatorelli*

# Chapter 17: Shark Scissors

*If there's something you always wanted to do, do it!*
*You have my permission, darling.*

After living *Sex in the City* single for years in New York, I married at
the tender age of thirty-eight, to Janet's surprise and delight. As time
passed, my husband Peter and I both began to tire of the daily grind,
so we planned ways to get away for a while. To my amusement, I got
an inspirational call the week before my fortieth birthday. It was Janet
and she was crying hysterically.

"Well, hello, Mom." I was quite used to her calling in tears. "How
are you?"

"You're going to be forty!" she screamed.

"Uh, yes, it's my birthday next week. So why is that so bad?" I
pulled the phone away from my ear just in time.

"THAT MEANS I'M OLD! Don't you dare say you're 40! For God's
sake, get a new driver's license and a boob job! Quick!"

"Well..."

"I'm coming up. I've scheduled us a Botox treatment and maybe
we can squeeze in a facelift for next week!"

*At least she didn't say nose job. Oh, wait a minute...facelift?*

"I've got the best nose job doctor in New York, Henry Hardbaw.
The stars all go to him."

*Oh, she did say nose job.*

"Mom," I comforted her, "you look fine. And so do I, incidentally..."

"Fine is for old maids. I need to look fabulous and we need to find
that rich man for you. And I can't do it at seventy. You need to get that

party going or we're both lost!"

"You know I'm already married, Janet."

"No matter. You need to take action now!"

Despite what Janet thought, I was married to a good guy and living in a shoebox apartment in NYC. For my fortieth birthday, my husband had something great planned, Paris. But after years in the concrete jungle, suffering the noise, dirt, stress and heat of the city, I wanted to do only one thing—go to the beach for my birthday. It was like answering a primordial call of the wild.

Janet had purchased a townhouse in the Panhandle of Florida a few years after my father had sadly died of bladder cancer in 1998. It was a devastating fight for over a year, with two unsuccessful surgeries, chemo, and the false hope of treatment after treatment. To watch him slowly die while being totally helpless was an anguish I had never known. Bill was seventy-five when he passed. I was only thirty-six years old. We were both too young.

With the rock of the family gone, it left a huge void in our hearts. My mother loved my dad dearly. She was there with him, all the way, even in his last days of life, taking care of him and fighting doctors, surgeons, small cell cancer, and anything else that got in the way of my father's health, but soon Janet realized even she was no match for the harsh disease. Of course we kept our sense of humor, as much as possible. Dad was quite a ham himself, putting on accents, telling jokes to visitors and, of course, acting in the theater group when he could. He loved to mimic Danny Kaye's routines, like the 1947 hit song, "Anatole of Paris" from the movie *The Secret Life of Walter Mitty*. He was amazing. Comedy had been (even though he discouraged me from my interest in it) important to him. Fittingly, the night before he passed, Dad's favorite British comedy sitcom, *Are You Being Served*, was playing on the television next to his bed. We watched as the blue glow of the set and canned laughter gently eased my father to another place.

Janet dealt with my father's cancer with strength, and naturally, a few Janet-esque moments. As ill as Dad became, the lesson learned from cancer had often escaped her as she'd steal a puff of two from her notorious Kools cigarettes in the hospital bathroom as my father lay in a coma on the bed a few feet away.

"Are you smoking?" demanded the no-nonsense nurse in a thick Jamaican accent as she banged on the bathroom door. "I can smell it all the way down the hall!"

"No, dear," Janet replied, and I knew from experience she was likely trying to blow the smoke down the toilet, conveniently forgetting that smoke rises.

"You have to stop. It's against the law!" She shook the doorknob.

"I'm almost out, don't worry."

"Do you know where you are? You are in a cancer ward! Are you mad?"

"No, darling, just damn tired, now, I put it out. That was my last one goddamit!" Janet fumed, literally.

I'm sure Dad was smiling under the morphine as the nurse stormed off. Yet, it was not nearly as bad as during Dad's funeral service when Janet stopped the entire procession along the cemetery road because she refused to go straight to the grave without making a stop at the chapel. The whole line of black limos lay in wait as Janet got out of her car and walked up to the funeral director with Bill's casket poked out of the back of the hearse.

"Stop!" We arranged for Bill to be at the chapel, you goddamed idiots! I swear I brought him here, and I'll take him back, you sons of bitches!"

Ah, if only she could.

So the sandy white beaches of Pensacola trumped the grand Eiffel Tower, the Parisian streets full of culture, and even a paying gig at the Improv. After years of city life and still mourning my father's death, I needed the sunshine. We delayed our pre-planned trip to Paris and hopped a plane to sunny Florida where we would visit my mother and the beach, and not necessarily in that order.

Janet's house was, as expected, a showcase of opulence. Because she regretted not living in Boca where "her people"—aka the wealthy and powerful—lived, she designed the interior in the spirit of compatriot, Joan Rivers: leopard curtains, ornate black marble bathrooms and countertops, and gold furnishings and fixtures everywhere. Her patio furniture was so bright it could be seen from space along with the Nazca lines in Peru.

Once we arrived, I found that every sheet, cushion, pot, pan, paint color, toothpick, and picture frame was designer-made. Her dry cleaning bill alone was $5,000 a month—and that was just for the napkins. And her clothes...the rows and rows that lined the walk-in closets did not disappoint. Hello, Fashion Week Pensacola.

And, even though I was forty, married, and living on my own, Janet remained obsessed with dressing me. Okay, why did I think Plaza Janet would be a vacation? On every visit she tried to push a raincoat, an '80s bulky blazer, or some over-the-top silk leopard scarf, jacket, or loud print on me.

"What are you wearing?" she looked me over as I walked in her door.

"Happy birthday to me." I rolled my eyes as I hugged her. I hadn't even set my bags down.

"I have all your clothes for the week laid out in your room and tomorrow is our first beach extravaganza!" She ran off to heat the curlers. My husband headed out that day, understandably, for drinking and skydiving in Flora-Bama (a strange nether world located between Florida and Alabama). It was full-on mother-daughter time which, while exhausting, was always an adventure.

The next afternoon, I found myself on Pensacola Beach, under an umbrella, sipping a piña colada. Ah, this is more like it. Janet was next to me, sipping her Martini, wearing a gold Dolce & Gabbana one-piece bathing suit with a matching metallic sun visor. She looked like a 1950s movie star and she knew it. The sheer reflective force of her outfit practically guided ships and planes to our location and held unsuspecting beachgoers in a trance. The calm of the Emerald Coast, its water routinely rolling on crystal white sand, seemed to have little effect on our starlet. Peering over her drink with a vengeance, she actively scanned the beach for "rich men," right down to the bulge in the side pocket. Janet was all about the wallet.

"Darling," she said, attacking one unsuspecting male. "Where do you summer?"

"Excuse me, ma'am?" questioned the boy.

"Never mind. Wait, who's your father? What does he do? I have a daughter who was in Second City and..."

"Mom...please..." I shook my head.

"May I adjust your umbrella, ma'am?" the cabana boy, probably a young kid in college, asked politely.

"Hardly," retorted Janet, already on the search for new prey.

After some serious sun, I decided to go for a swim. On the way to the water, I was surprised when my yellow bikini attracted a few whistles, but found I was no match for Janet's gold metallic swimwear. Janet waded into the clear water with me, straining her neck to avoid getting her hair wet. Swimming with her daughter was fun for her as long as her looks were not compromised. She had also heard saltwater might neutralize the effects of Botox.

"Mom," I urged, "swim, put your head under."

"Swim?" Janet was shocked. "Why would I go to the beach to swim? It's as if you don't even know me, darling."

As I was ready to plunge underwater, a scream rang out only a few feet away.

"Shark!" cried a lady, her visor slipping down over her sun-blocked face. Filled with fear, she slashed violently at the waves. Like the *Jaws* panic in Montauk, Long Island, terrified tourists leapt for the safety of the shoreline. The lifeguards, in turn, ran to the surf, their red water-floaties at the ready. In reality, it was more like a bad scene from *Baywatch,* David Hasselhoff probably lurking nearby.

I started to make my own mad dash up the beach when I turned around. Janet was still in the water. Her hand went straight up in the air, and I saw a gold streak flash down into the surf. Janet then grabbed a kid by the seat of his trunks and pulled him to the shore. *What in the world?* I thought, staring at the shining object in Janet's hand. A crowd gathered, amazed that this sexy, mysterious seventy-year-old blonde had risen from the water with a young boy in one hand, and a sharp object of unknown origin in the other.

Fortunately our predator turned out to just be a small, one-foot sand shark, but the crowd was no less impressed. Janet worked in some classic poses, of course, while folks took pictures with her and the awe-struck boy. Cell phones didn't quite have that snappy paparazzi camera sound, she reasoned, but they would suffice. Then I heard her whisper in his ear, "By the way, honey, what does *your* father do?"

The boy thanked her and politely pulled away and ran to his family. Shaking herself off, Janet returned to our umbrella and chairs where she gulped down the rest of her tepid Martini. "Ah! I love the view at this beach! Not one bulge has gotten past me. Don't give up hope, darling."

"Mom! That was amazing!" I said, shaking my head. "I saw something in your hand out in the water?"

"Shark scissors, darling." She pulled a pair of gold scissors from the trendy belt on her hip.

"I always carry them on yachting excursions and alterations appointments. Actually, I hardly ever leave home without 'em."

You learn something new every day, even about your own mother.

The following day Janet's photo made the *Pensacola News Journal*, and yes, on the fashion page. Once again, Janet was in the news. Although her heroism and creative thinking in a crisis were mentioned in the cutline, the photo highlighted her gold Dolce & Gabbana suit and its matching accessories, sun visor and shark scissors. There was Janet posing with the lifeguards, her leg balanced gracefully up in the air, the signature pose for our local celebrity. The picture looked all too familiar.

And I'd never been prouder of Janet Lee or more perplexed. It would seem Pensacola might hold promise of a great future for our little heroine and after all, we'll always have Paris.

Ok, maybe we won't.

Janet posing at a Pensacola pool

# Chapter 18: A Bum Rap

*If you simply must wear orange, make it Versace!*

"Hey, where are you going?" cried Janet Lee, shaking her fist through the cold bars of the Santa Rosa County jail cell. She had been locked up for thirty minutes.

The deputy who was walking by stopped and turned. After a long pause, he said, "The bathroom…"

"Don't leave me with him!" cried Janet, pointing her red-nailed finger at the deputy guarding the prisoners. "I'll get defiled!"

Janet was indeed a jailbird that Friday night and being a fairly recent widow, she attempted a little something called "dating." After a quick drink on the beach with her new friend, whose last name was actually "Gonads," Janet had decided he didn't appeal to her (probably due to his lack of them). As a result, on her way home, the law had apparently caught her allegedly veering off the road. Therefore, in a flash, two deputies picked her up only five minutes from the safety of her front door in Gulf Breeze. Outraged that she had been stopped at all, Janet refused to blow into the Breathalyzer. "Who else has blown on that? Get that germ-ridden thing away from me!"

To make matters worse, when she performed the "walk and tape test," instead of walking in a straight line, Janet got one of her three-inch heels caught on the sticky side of the tape she was supposed to follow and fell over onto the hood of the deputy's car. The "evil" Deputy Sherman T. Thistlewaite, as she later told me, then cuffed her, kicking and screaming, and took her to the county jail in Milton, Florida. From the back seat of the car, all the way to the cell, Janet threatened to tear her clothes off and cry "rape" if they didn't take her back home. She even threatened to have their "f-ing jobs" if they didn't release her. As irate as she was about getting pulled over, she became even more incensed when she arrived at the jail. Two female deputies handed her a set of bright orange PJs, especially designed for her stay.

"I haven't even been proven guilty. You bastards!" she protested. "I'm not getting into that ridiculous orange jumpsuit." They told her it would make the other inmates feel better if she changed.

"Feel better? *Springing them* would make them feel better," she retorted.

They cajoled her for two and a half hours before she reluctantly changed out of her wrap-around skirt, silk blouse, and Anne Klein suit to embrace her new ghastly-orange reality. Livid with the captors who had forced her to adopt this hideous new look, Janet continued to cuss them out all night long. The only break she gave them was the short time she chatted with another prisoner they had put in with her.

Deputy Thistlewaite—apparently notorious for nabbing blondes off the highway to meet ticket quotas—had picked up quite a few folks that night. Alcohol was big business, it seemed, in the then-dry county. Janet's temporary cellmate, Shirley, a brassy blonde, had also been picked for driving under the influence. She had bloodshot eyes, smelled of booze, and looked like a younger version of Janet Lee. And Shirley was definitely "drunk." She even admitted it and compared it to other times she had been arrested for prostitution and even littering.

From what I was told, the two of them had a great time "raisin' hell" in their cell and recanting their inmate stories. The girls had the most fun discussing which deputies were the most attractive. "That stud at booking" clearly won the contest. And the obvious acne problem and "skanky ass" breath of Deputy Thistlewaite made him come in last.

"I'll have that bastard's job before the sun comes up," Janet announced with confidence. She ranted on and on to Shirley, to the "creepy" deputy on duty, to the entire incarcerated population, and to anyone else who walked by, about the injustice that had been done to her. Evidently, she had never seen the TV special *Scared Straight.*

"Hello, boys!" she roared at some new guys they had picked up fresh off the streets. Janet became so loud that even some muscle-bound inmates in the cage across from her started to shush her. One prisoner who was on special duty mopping the floor made his way over to the girls' cellblock and looked directly at Janet.

"Ma'am, be quiet. They'll keep you in here forever."

"The hell I'll stay quiet! I'm gonna sue these jackasses. You look worn out. Want something to drink? I'll tell them to give you a soda."

"I'm fine, ma'am."

"You missed a spot." Janet laughed. "Don't get in trouble."

Janet and Shirley continued to yell, tell dirty jokes, and laugh themselves silly in their new PJs. They became so raucous the mean "lesbian" deputy, who had forced Janet to lose her fashion standing, eventually separated the two blondes. Janet ended up in solitary confinement until the bail bondsman sprung her the next morning.

A few months later, Janet was a full civilian once again and I worked to help her win her DUI court case—which I've heard, seldom happens in Santa Rosa County. Deputy Thistlewaite had arrested the wrong woman—or had indeed confused Janet's green eyes with Shirley's brown eyes on the arrest report. And Janet's "person" did not "reek of booze." She even presented the clothes she'd worn that night to the judge who she had approached, against her lawyer's advice, before the trial.

"Judge Evans, darling, it's so nice to meet you!"

"Ma'am, you can't talk to me." The judge shook his head, a bit taken aback.

"Well, I know you're going to do the right thing," she smiled. "Nice meeting you, Tom. See you in court!"

I managed to snag the official Santa Rosa County Arrest Report before she was exonerated.

I thought maybe it would come in handy one day...like right now.

PW/PRO    0-9

**ARREST REPORT**
**REPORT NO:** ▓▓▓▓▓▓▓▓

SANTA ROSA COUNTY SHERIFFS OFFICE

| Jail Booking No | Offense No | Other No | OBTS ▓▓▓▓ |
|---|---|---|---|

**[ SUSPECT ]**

| Last | First | Middle | Title | Race | Sex | DOB | Age | Hgt | Wgt |
|---|---|---|---|---|---|---|---|---|---|
| ▓▓ | JANET | ▓▓ | | W | F | 9/4/1932 | 71 | 5'05" | 140 |

| Eyes | Hair | MNI Number | SSN | I.D. No. | St | Type | OCA/Agency ID |
|---|---|---|---|---|---|---|---|
| BRO | BLN | ▓▓ | ▓▓ | ▓▓ | FL | | |

Birth Location: City: County: State: Nation: Citizenship:
Addresses (Current/Last Known is Listed First)
▓▓ Apt/Lot: GULF BREEZE FL 32563 Phone: 850 Entered: 3/31/2004
Occupations (Current/Last Known is Listed First)
* none found in MNI *
Aliases (Last, First Middle Title DOB)
* none found in MNI *
Street Names
* none found in MNI *

**[ INCIDENT INFORMATION ]**

| Occurred Date Range: 3/31/2004 | 21:07 | to 3/31/2004 | 21:07 | | |
|---|---|---|---|---|---|
| No. | Di Street | Apt/Lot City | ST Zip | (GEO) | |
| | | GULF BREEZE | FL 325 | 1 - 01 - 0 - | |

**[ CHARGES ]**

316.193.2a TRAFFIC OFFENSE
DUI ALCOHOL OR DRUGS 1ST OFF

| Counts | Level | Degree | GOC | UCR | NCIC | AON |
|---|---|---|---|---|---|---|
| 1 | Misdemeanor | Second | Not Applicable | 5400 | | 5499 |

318.14. RESIST OFFICER
REFUSE TO ACCEPT SIGN CITATION OR POST BOND

| Counts | Level | Degree | GOC | UCR | NCIC | AON |
|---|---|---|---|---|---|---|
| 1 | Misdemeanor | Second | Not Applicable | 9000 | | 4801 |

**[ STATEMENT OF PROBABLE CAUSE / NARRATIVE ]**

On 3/31▓ while traveling south on College I saw a white four door Cadillac bearing Florida tag ▓▓ driving half in the turn lane and half in the south bound lane. As I was catching up to the vehicle, it turned east on to Santa Rosa Drive and began to go up the hill driving east bound in the west bound lane. I initiated my lights to effect a traffic stop at which time a vehicle which was coming west bound had to go half way off the road and the white Cadillac swerved in to the east bound lane. The vehicle continued east bound on Santa Rosa Dr until it got to the stop sign at Bayview Ln.

I met with the driver, later identified as Janet ▓▓. While talking with Ms ▓▓ I noted very slurred and mumbled speech, blood shot, watery eyes and the strong smell of an alcoholic beverage coming from her breath and person.

Dep ▓▓ arrived on scene and while telling him what I had Ms ▓▓ exited her vehicle and came back to where we were at. While talking with Ms ▓▓ she had to use my left arm three times for support and I asked her if she had been drinking. Ms ▓▓ stated that she had four small glasses of wine and agreed to perform the field sobriety tasks (FST's) when I asked her if she would do them.

Ms ▓▓ only did part of the horizontal gaze nystagmus and while attempting to explain how to do the walk and turn Ms ▓▓ walked down the line, ran into the front of my parol car and fell over the hood. On the second attempt of explaining she walked past the tape end and began to walk to the drivers door of her vehicle. I stopped her as she was reaching for the door handle of the drivers door and placed her under arrest for DUI.

Dep ▓▓ waited for the tow service and I transported Ms Trojan to the Santa Rosa County Jail.

Printed On: ▓▓ 2004 11:26:48 PM

# SANTA ROSA COUNTY ARREST REPORT

OFFENSE REPORT

SANTA ROSA COUNTY SHERIFFS OFFICE
Printed On: 04/01/2004 at 12:46

CAD INCIDENT DISPOSITION CODE: [72-1] [ 1T] [ 4] [ ]

On ██████ at I turned off of Hwy 98 on to College Dr south bound I saw a white Cadillac in front of me driving half way in the turn lane and half way in the south bound lane. I began to catch up with the vehicle which turned left on to Santa Rosa Dr driving east in the west bound lane going up the hill on Santa Rosa Dr. I initiated my lights at this time and as I was catching up to the vehicle a vehicle that was west bound had to leave the roadway by half its car and the white Cadillac swerved into the east bound lane of Santa Rosa Dr. The vehicle was a 2000 Cadillac four door, white in color, bearing Florida tag ████████. The vehicle continued east bound on Santa Rosa Dr and began to drive down the middle of the roadway. The vehicle continued east bound until it got to the stop sign at Santa Rosa Dr and Bayview Ln at which time the driver stopped.

I met with the driver, later identified as Janet ██████████, and asked for her drivers license. Ms ██████ asked why I had stopped her and I explained that she was driving down the wrong side of the road and almost had an accident after she had turned on to Santa Rosa Dr. Ms ██████ stated that she did not almost have an accident and that she was only a block from her house and for me to please let her be on her way. Ms ██████ finally located her drivers license in her purse and when she handed it to me she also handed me her AAA card, which I told her I did not need and returned it to her. While talking with Ms ██████ noted she had very slurred and mumbled speech, blood shot, watery eyes and the strong smell of an alcoholic beverage coming from her breath and person. I told Ms ██████ to stay in her vehicle while I checked her drivers license.

I went to my patrol car to run Ms ██████'s drivers license and requested unit 108, Dep██████, to be en route to assist me on this stop. Dep ██████ arrived on scene and I was explaining to him what occurred and while I was explaining to him Ms ██████ exited her vehicle and began to walk back toward us. Ms ██████ was unsteady on her feet and when she got to me she asked how long this was going to take. I explained to Ms ██████ that I thought that she was impaired and asked her if she had been drinking. She stated that she had four small glasses of wine and that was all she had drank. While talking with Ms ██████ she grabbed my left arm three times to maintain her balance. I asked Ms ██████ if she would perform several field sobriety tasks (FST's) and she stated, "I'm almost home, can't you just call PK". I explained to her no and asked her if she would perform the FST's and she agreed.

The first task I instructed/performed was the horizontal gaze nystagmus task. I had to remind Ms ██████ twice to keep her head still and after doing the maximum deviation, which I saw distinct nystagmus in both left and right eyes, Ms ██████ looked directly at me and would not follow my thumb which I was using as a stimulus.

I placed a piece of yellow duct tape approximately 15' long between my patrol car and her vehicle for the remainder of the tasks. I asked Ms ██████ to stand on the tape facing my patrol car in the instructional position at which time she walked the tape in normal strides and fell over on top of the hood of my car. I again explained to Ms ██████ to just get in the instructional position and not do anything until I told her to. She began to get on the tape then walked down the tape line, past the tape line and began to walk toward the drivers door of her vehicle. I stopped Ms ██████ as she was reaching for the drivers door handle at which time I placed her under arrest for DUI.

Dep ██████ stood by for Bayside Towing to tow the vehicle and I transported Ms ██████ to the Santa Rosa County Jail.

While en route to the Santa Rosa County Jail Ms ██████ advised me that she knew the Governor of Kentucky, they were close friends and that she was a Colonel in the Kentucky Guard. Ms ██████ also stated for me to call PK for him to come get her and take her home. She also stated that I had no right to arrest her, that she was going to have my "fucking job" and sue my "sorry ass". She also advised that I was a "sorry excuse for an officer", that I needed to call Gov Bush because he is a close friend of hers and for me to just take her home so I would not get into trouble. She also stated that if I did not turn around she would jump out of the car and kill herself and that would ruin her life and my career. Ms ██████ also stated that when she got to the jail or met with her lawyer she was going to say that I had raped her and that no body could prove she was lying and that my "fucking job" would be history. Ms ██████ repeated all these things above several times all the way to the jail.

After arriving at the Santa Rosa County Jail Ms ██████ gave the booking officers a problem by not doing what

S█████████ | DLL ██████ 22:42 |

117

# SANTA ROSA COUNTY ARREST REPORT

*OFFENSE REPORT*  SANTA ROSA COUNTY SHERIFFS OFFICE

Printed On: 04/01/200■ @ 12:46

was asked and then they brought her into the intoxilyzer room after she was booked into the Jail. I began my 20 minute observation period at 2145 hours while en route to the jail. At 2202 hours I requested Ms ▓▓ perform the breath test and she refused. At 2204 hours I read Implied Consent and Ms ▓▓ refused to perform the breath test. Ms ▓▓ stated that I had no right to arrest her, this was a false arrest, she was not DUI and that I had kidnapped her and falsely imprisoned her and she was going to have my job.

At 2209 hours I read Miranda and Ms ▓▓ refused to answer any questions. After completing the DUI citation, #▓▓, and the written warning, #▓▓, for not maintaining a single lane I asked Ms ▓▓ to sign the citations and she refused. I explained to Ms ▓▓ signing was not an admission of guilt, but that she had received a citation and if she refused to sign she could be charged with refusing to sign a citation. Ms ▓▓ declined to sign the citation and was issued citation # 1039-CBB9 for refusing to sign DUI citation.

I completed all paperwork in this matter. This incident occurred in Santa Rosa County, Florida.

< END OF NARRATIVE >

| Offense Status | Yes -- Cleared | | Reporting Officer |
|---|---|---|---|
| Closed | # Clearances | 1 | 054 ▓▓ |
| | Clearance Date | 03/3▓ | SHF/CHF/MAJ/OPS/PATROL/D1 |
| Warr./Arr. No. | Clearance Type | Arrest | |
| | Except. Clear. Type | | *Forward for Approval / Followup To : |
| | Age Classification | ADULT | |

| Date Entered NCIC: | | Date Removed NCIC: | |

| Supervisor | APPROVED | | | | Case Screening Supv. | Investigator |
|---|---|---|---|---|---|---|
| | | Yes | Concur | No | | |
| Date | Time | No | PdF/U | No | Date | Time |
| 04/01/2004 | 12:37 | No | InvF/U | No | | |

Report Last Modified 04/01/200■ 12:37

| DLL    03/31/200■ 22:42 |

118

# Chapter 19: Driving Miss Diva

*If you can work a runway, you can goddamn well work a courtroom!*

The small back road was only four miles from Janet's townhouse in Gulf Breeze. We stopped to survey the scene of her "non-crime." One thing I noticed was that they claimed Janet crossed the yellow line in the road while driving. A week after the arrest, Janet and I embarked on a little detective work.

As we left it, Janet could not drive because of her notorious DUI arrest and famed altercations with the cast of the Milton Jail. She got an attorney, Art Rezmon, to right the wrongs committed, and I helped her prepare her case against the notorious Deputy Thistlewaite. We wanted to make sure she was vindicated during her day in court.

"There's no goddamn yellow line! Bastards! I had to drive in the middle, there was no road left." They had held Janet overnight in jail. I was still in New York at the time. Fortunately, a nice bail bondsman took her home at five o'clock in the morning. She of course found out his life story and he, in turn, was shocked they even picked her up in the first place.

We both got out of my car for closer examination of exhibit #1. The edge of the road dropped sharply off the side, just enough to have caused some major fender damage. Most folks hovered in toward the middle for good measure. And Janet was right, there was definitely no yellow line.

"Couldn't have said it better, Mom." I took a picture of the unlined road.

A few months later, her courthouse debut was upon us. Over that time, we had noticed they had repainted the dim yellow line to a bright, shiny yellow. Too late, we had snapped the evidence pic of the questionable line, the smoking gun if you will.

Janet went to the courthouse wearing the outfit she was arrested in, not dry cleaned, to prove it did not "reek of booze." We entered the county building in Milton, Florida, located the courtroom and quickly took our seats. *If these walls could talk*, I thought looking around at the stark atmosphere, thinking of an episode of the Florida-based reality show, *The People's Court*.

"How droll this place is. Which judge is presiding today?" Janet asked one of the clerks passing by. She had apparently brushed up on her legal lingo.

"Judge Maloney," he said, giving us a backwards glance.

Art, Janet's attorney, finally met them in the hall in front of the courtroom. He was shaking for some reason.

"Who are we up against?" she asked Art.

Art pointed to four men standing in circle talking a few feet away. Janet went straight to them. "Excuse me, are you Judge Maloney?"

One of the men turned to her and motioned at his somber black robe.

"I have been waiting ninety long days and nights to see you," she continued. Janet eagerly took his hand and shook it. "I am so happy to meet you. It's just about over. I couldn't even drive myself to get beer and cigarettes!" Janet leaned in so close to him that she practically kissed him on the cheek. Gasps were heard in the crowd. Art quickly gathered Janet and guided her to safety.

"Uh, yes, nice to meet you, Miss Conley. Now you better get in the courtroom..." Judge Maloney had apparently not dealt with someone as bold as my mother.

"Judge, it's been a pleasure meeting you and I look forward to you finding me innocent." Beads of sweat formed on Art's brow and he stuttered an apology for his client, but Janet was undeterred. "Be fair now," she advised as Art guided her away. "Oh, and which one of you is the prosecutor?"

Art was shaking like a food processor and Janet pointed toward him with her thumb. "Why is my lawyer a nervous wreck?"

"Mom, can't you tell, he's an alcoholic."

"Let's call it simpatico, darling." She then approached the prosecutor.

"I understand you're going to prosecute me? Well, I'm going to beat you. Get ready to be beaten because I'm going to win this case. I'm innocent," she proclaimed with measured confidence like she was Sharon Stone in *Basic Instinct*.

"You're the next case up? You're not supposed to be talking to me," he forcefully whispered.

"Yes, you're prosecuting me. My attorney is Art Rezmon, and you don't want to mess with us!"

You could hear Art gulp from across the hallway.

"I'm going to have to ask you not to address me directly," the prosecutor insisted.

"Oh, don't flatter yourself. See you in court." Janet waved.

After a few minutes of wondering what was to become of Janet, we all situated ourselves in the courtroom. And so court was called to order. The cops took the stand first and Art approached the bench.

"Do you know who put the sticker yellow tape down on the ground?"

"I don't recall," replied Deputy Thistlewaite. Her nemesis, in the flesh, seemed a lot less threatening than that fateful night three months ago. Before Art could proceed, he heard a chair slide across the floor.

"I do!" Janet shouted, standing up for emphasis.

"Order in the court," the judge banged the gavel.

"Ok, darling," Janet cooed and eased back down in her seat, carefully readjusting her clothes as the men stared on. Soon, it was her turn to take the stand. "Your honor, they said my clothes smelled like alcohol and vomit. Can you imagine? Do I look like someone who would allow that to happen? Here, smell my clothes." Janet presented her sweater, scarf, and heels in the bag. "I'm wearing the suit that I wore that fateful night, and even though it was very difficult, I refrained from having it dry cleaned until today."

Nervous Art had pointed out that the description in the police report better described the woman who shared the jail cell with Janet, the one who was stone drunk, smelling of booze.

Janet pointed out that the high heels that she wore that night were old and the heeltap was pulled off by the adhesive tape the officers had ordered her to walk on. "It's a good brand, your honor, but the heel came off when tape was put down. It wouldn't stick because the wind blew the tape over and wouldn't stay flat on the ground. So he called the other cop over to help hold it down. I definitely recall. So when I was called up to walk on it, it was as twisted as a French braid, your honor. And that's why my taps were taken off by the tape. See?" She showed the shoes. "And another thing, that yellow line, there wasn't one."

"That's right your honor, here is the evidence." Art approached the judge and presented the pictures we took.

"That was taken by my daughter, Leanna. She's so talented…and she's single too. If any of you nice gentlemen—"

The judge cut her off. "Ms. Conley that will be enough."

There was a smattering of giggles in the courtroom as I slowly sunk back into my seat. I looked over to my left and saw the husky bailiff wink at me. *Good Lord*, I thought as I heard Janet continue undeterred.

"So, Mr. Judge, as you can clearly see, my heels came clean off. So please tell me how any lady, even one who had a day and a half of charm school and an early career on the catwalks of Chicago…" she looked over at the judge, pointed to herself and mouthed, *that would be me* "…so I ask you judge, who could walk a straight line under those conditions? Do you know how hard it is to walk in three-inch heels as it is, much less on a sticky surface, darling?"

Art motioned at Janet with a subtle slide of his hand over his throat.

"Art, dear, don't worry. You are such a worrywart. I just want this nice, sweet judge to understand what I had to go through that night. You understand now, don't you, Judge?"

Janet smiled and batted her obviously green eyes at the judge who sat in stunned silence for a moment before saying, "The officer mentioned that you were a member of some sort of club…"

"Well your honor…" Art began.

Janet interrupted, "What he's talking about is that I'm a Kentucky

Colonel. In case you haven't heard of it, it's quite an honor to be a member and it's made up of people who have been acknowledged for helping the good people of Kentucky. It could be a heroic deed, public service, or being a generous benefactor, like yours truly. In fact, here's my membership card signed by the governor himself. If it pleases the court, I honorably submit that I am not the type to be arrested. I have dear friends and family members who are senators, judges, and lawyers. I come from a law-abiding lineage with a great respect for due process. So in conclusion, I was not drunk and that confused officer made a terrible, terrible mistake."

She paused for a moment and then added, "Oh, and I forgive him."

The judge stared at her for a minute before reading from the report. "You did fall over the hood of the police car…"

"Who wouldn't, your honor, with broken heels, wind gusting, poor visibility…seriously, how stable would you be?"

"You also said, 'If you don't let me out of this (expletive) car I'll have you incarcerated for attempted rape.'" The judge held the report closer to his bifocals for a better look.

"Well, my brother is a cop and that's what he told me to say. Your honor, it was the middle of the night and I did not know these people. I was a few minutes from home and instead of escorting me home they cuffed me."

Art leapt up, reminding everyone that he was still there. "And, your honor, my client refused the Breathalyzer test only after she understandably tripped from the sticky tape that caught her broken heel. None are admissible in court so we do not know what her alcohol level actually was."

Janet reached over and lightly tapped the judge on his arm. "I didn't want to put my mouth on anything they carried around in that car," she said, scrunching up her face. "They didn't even read me my Amanda Rights!"

Art joined in. "She means Miranda Rights, and they didn't administer them as they should have."

"Damn right!" piped up Janet. "Where are my god..uh, Miranda Rights?"

"And there was no erratic driving because there were no yellow lines for her to cross. They had faded and she was forced to guess. She was merely trying to keep her vehicle on this narrow road at night. And her eyesight isn't what it used…"

"I think he gets the point," Janet said sternly.

"Uh, I rest our case." Art sat back down.

After a long ten minutes, the judge came out of his chambers. "We find the defendant, Janet Lee Conley Trojan, not guilty of driving under the influence. Case dismissed." The judge banged the gavel.

"YES!" Everyone cheered. Once again, Janet had her audience enrapt.

Janet strutted out of that courthouse like Erin Brockovich saving the community from tainted water, giving Thistlewaite one last backward glance of victory. You could see his overwhelming expression of relief as we passed by.

Equally elated, Art invited us over to his house for a nightcap, of all things. After Janet and Art downed a few Martinis, we called it a night. As the designated driver, I took Janet home. She got out of the car, shimmied out of her suit, and tossed it through the car window.

"Would you be a love and drop this off at the cleaners?"

# Chapter 20: A Stent in Time

*The hotter the cop, the sweeter the arrest!*
*Cuff me, darling! I've got all day!*

I had only been down to visit my mom from New York City a few times since she landed in Florida in 2000. In 2004, the summer of Hurricane Ivan, I was still married, hacking away at my comedy career, and welcomed yet another visit to the Sunshine State. By hacking (a term sometimes used for comics) I mean I was working in a mid-town law firm during the day and hustling over to the Broadway Comedy Club at night to emcee (draining), or do a unpaid "spot" for five minutes (more draining) or even worse, be a part of a little scheme called "barking." That's where a club owner's favorite comic runs the room for the night and has you (the non-favorite comic) at their mercy as you "bark" or stand in the freezing cold usually on a city street corner handing out flyers to indifferent passersby. "Come see the show with comics from *Letterman* and HBO". We would exaggerate our tiny credits into an impressive sales pitch. Chances were, however, that once we dragged someone in off the street they usually wasted no time making a swift getaway.

Yet, I had done this "stage time" drill on and off for ten years, even producing shows to get my own stage time under control, but even that was tedious. Slowly, over the years, I worked at comedy clubs on the East Coast (Broadway Comedy Club, Zanies and the Laugh Factory), was one of the first female writers way back when for *Dennis Miller Live*, pitched to Comedy Central, and produced my own TV pilots. I even had a few decent reviews in local papers, but stand up is an endurance game and I was exhausted. To make matters worse, Janet was practically a fugitive, so I figured I better head back to Florida and keep tabs on her.

Taking advantage of the great weather one afternoon, I decided it was time for Janet and me to play a rousing game of tennis at Santa Rosa public courts. After about three volleys, I realized that my little spitfire was running out of gas. She fainted in her tight little twenty-five-year-old Diane Von Furstenberg tennis skirt (which admittedly could be suffocating). Three hours later I was at her bedside at Sacred Heart Hospital in Pensacola. Janet was sporting her designer sunglasses, in a hospital gown, kicking her leg up in the air as they wheeled her down the glaring hallway en route to get her first heart stent, which I was not looking forward to.

Janet has had a lifelong history with doctors. Her seventh colonoscopy almost killed her...not because of complications from the surgery, but the doctor overdosed her anesthesia when Janet demanded he wake her up before he removed any polyps.

"This is going to hurt you a lot more than me." He jabbed her in the rear end with a syringe full of knockout drugs. Janet barely survived the ordeal.

And during one of her many endoscopies, our family doctor sedated the little starlet, only for her groggily to reveal during the procedure to the doctor, nurses, and my father that she wanted to give JFK oral gratification.

Camelot, indeed.

Or we could mention the time I was being measured for breast implants and she told the plastic surgeon, "Darling, date my daughter," mid-nipple.

Ah, the best of times...

"This could be exciting! I wonder if they make designer heart valves. This is one time I could use that J. Crew yuppie look." The Valium in her system was apparently taking hold. The stern nurse started to administer an extra dose of sedative.

"Darling, if you're going to pick a vein, make it on my bad side. Don't cut me open anywhere near my face."

"Mrs. Conley, you do know we're putting the stent in through your leg."

"Leg, face, it's all the same, darling. By the way, when's the last time you used blush? You look pale as a sheet. Never cover the pretty when you can reinforce with makeup, my dear."

Four hours later, Janet woke up out of the fog and realized she could breathe a lot easier, literally. They had inserted three small heart stents. The doctor pulled me aside and showed me the x-rays—a 70% blockage in one artery and a 90% blockage in the other. Truly life-threatening heart disease had been occurring, and being she was a heavy smoker, and one of her favorite dietary supplements was pork rinds, I could understand why we were having this crisis. That day on the tennis court could have been the final chapter of The Daily Janet.

Recovering after heart surgery, Janet was not in a gaming mood. She complained about the food, the dressing gown, and of course, me. She pointed out how my career hadn't flourished as she had hoped. Somehow whenever she started listing her disappointments, I got lumped in. With her insults reaching an all-time high I decided this was a good time to say farewell. I assured her that I'd be back tomorrow (if I could muster the strength and shore up my defenses).

The next day Janet awoke with tubes and wires emanating from over her body. Plus, she was hungry, bored, and apparently out of cigarettes. Last but not least, the nurses wouldn't even let her bum a few smokes.

"Kelly, dear...thanks for the pudding, but what about my Virginia Slims?"

"You just had heart stents."

"I know. I'm feeling great. Thanks. By the way, how much purple can you wear every day...a tad nauseating, don't you think?" That was Janet, asking for a favor on the one hand and dishing out unwarranted advice on the other, which seemed totally acceptable to her.

The nurse slammed the door.

"Really!" Janet couldn't bear it another minute. She jumped up from her adjustable-rail bed with wires, IV and all in tow, and high-tailed it to the parking lot. She jumped into her Cadillac and headed to the nearby Circle K convenience store for a Budweiser and some cigs. Janet screeched out of the parking garage, bands on her wrists, and butt naked on the cold leather driver's seat on a mission. On her hospital bed she had left only a silver compact and a whiff of Chanel No. 5.

"What you need, honey?" the clerk asked my mother.

"Oh hello, Deidra, the usual, Virginia Slims menthol and a six pack of Bud. I'll just throw in a few Snickers and some pork rinds…"

"By the way, Janet, I took your advice and started wearing heels to work and now my sex life is great." Deidra smiled.

"With me!" A male voice sounded from behind the counter wall. It was her rather skinny stoner boyfriend, Duke. Also a clerk.

"Oh, fantastic!" Janet clapped her hands together. "Yes…a good pair of heels always slays 'em. You can't depend on the lottery, honey."

"Wanna f★★★?" A deep male voice uttered.

"I beg your pardon?" Janet exclaimed. She turned around to find a tough-looking man with a long beard, jeans, and a Fantastic Four t-shirt…in neon.

"I'm a hospital patient; does it look like I'm in the mood?" Janet waved her wires.

"Well, your ass is bare," he said looking down.

"OH!" She said quickly closing her hospital gown. "It was an emergency today. Maybe another time, darling." Janet scooted out of the Circle K as fast as possible and got into her Caddy just as a police car pulled into the parking lot. A good-looking officer walked up to her window.

"Mrs. Conley? You're supposed to be at the hospital."

"I know, darling. I was just on my way back, had to pick up some essentials. My, you're handsome…what's your name?"

"D.K."

"Oh, I love men with initials. Is there any chance you can just guide me home? It's right around the corner."

"Well, Miss Conley, you're not officially discharged from the hospital. You apparently left without telling anyone," D.K. stated.

"Rats, it just slipped my mind, stress, you know…" Janet smiled.

"Well, you can't do that."

"Oh, I'm so sorry, D.K. Please just take me home," she pleaded.

"How are you feeling? We may need to go back to the hospital."

"Fit as a fiddle. I love heart stents. Great stuff," Janet said.

"Ok, let me call in to the hospital. Please stay right here until I return."

"Yes, sir!" Janet put on some lip liner in the mirror and refreshed her makeup...even took off a few wires to make herself look more presentable. D.K. returned to find Janet in vamp mode, "Ready. I'll go back tomorrow for the compact I left there."

"I've informed security that you're fine and you elected to go home. They will want you back tomorrow to check you out."

"Hmm, sounds ducky."

Janet loved the attention she got as she followed the blinking lights of the police cruiser all the way home.

# Chapter 21: Mazel Tov, Darling

*Fame looks chic on anyone, darling! Wear it well!*

I was still in my NYC I'm-going-to-make-it, "Hossenfeffer Incorporated " phase when one Saturday afternoon I was having lunch with Janet at Sardis. She was on the lookout for celebrities. Thanks to her undeterred confidence, she was certain that I was destined to be a star, mainly based on the fact that I was the daughter whom she had spent her life grooming. I was twenty-nine and had been working as an editorial assistant in The Big Apple, and I'd even been an assistant to best-selling novelist Barbara Taylor Bradford. Janet loved the fact that I lived in New York, perusing her—I mean my dream to be a star. It made her feel like she had won, like her life, and her sacrifices had indeed been worth it. It was unspoken pressure that I was reminded of whenever she called or visited.

In the dank restaurant, we noshed as we took in the headshots of stars littering the walls and sat on worn red leather seats that had supported the asses of countless notables. The city car horns were muffled to an almost tolerable roar on the other side of the window and then in walks, of all people, a famous Jewish comedian I admire, we'll call him "FJC" for short, takes the table right next to us. Albeit some years ago, this is the gist of the conversation and subsequent meetings:

"Mom," I whispered. I knew she was aching to see celebrities and I had seen my fair share around town. I knew this would be a good spot for star spotting and sure enough, we hit pay dirt.

"Hello, darling." She was on it, leaning in for emphasis. FJC was known for holding court at many NYC establishments and even diners so this was surely nothing new for him.

He looked at her and said, "You talking to me?" The classic line was spoken.

"Why yes," said Janet.

FJC not missing a beat looked at us both and smiled. "Mind if I join you?"

"Not at all. So nice to meet you!" Janet had nabbed a famous comic and she was not going to squander this opportunity.

"And you are?" He turned to look directly at me.

"I'm Leanna," I answered.

"What do you do?" FJC asked.

"She's a stand-up comic," Janet blurted. Well, I guess it had to slip out sometime.

"Mom!" I wasn't sure I wanted to admit it.

"Ah, you are?" FJC smiled.

"Well, yes. I mean, I'm trying…" I wasn't going to claim headliner status.

"Don't try. You are, or you aren't."

"Thanks, Yoda!"

"You got it!" He laughed.

The conversation soon took a more serious turn. We talked about his time as a Rabbi, and how he felt about the comedy world, and what happens in life when you choose the path of comedy. In a way, he was like a sage who was destined to pass on his wisdom to me and I was soaking it up. He really was like Yoda. There are just some things you can't get from a book and this experience was one of them.

We were walking outside after our meal when he said to me, "Does your father approve of your career choice?"

"No, he wanted me to have a *real* career."

"It's very difficult when your father doesn't approve. When I gave up being a Rabbi, it was devastating to my parents. But I had to do it."

We just started to get to the meat of the issue and Janet, who had been interjecting our comedy discussion with modeling stories, boomed in. "Well, when are we going to see you again, darling? Here's

131

Leanna's number. Get her a part in something, will you?" For once, I didn't mind the forwardness.

"Anytime, Janet, I'm here every Tuesday." He politely took the number, but I knew he wasn't going to call. It was a professional courtesy, I assumed.

FJC wished me the best of luck. "Leanna, I'll be on Broadway in a few months. Take your dad to the show and bring him backstage. I'd like to meet him."

"Yes, I will. Thank you." I pictured Dad meeting FJC and suddenly he had a big smile of approval on his face, giving me a nod. Ah, to dream.

My father didn't visit me much in New York City, but when he did I tried, in whatever studio or semi-standard living conditions I had, to let him know I was on the right track. January is notoriously cold in New York, and it was the winter of 1994. The buildings emphasized the stark white nature, with spears jutting up into grayness. Poetic, yes. The broad marquee on 8th Avenue on the West Side was lit with the title: "Politically Incorrect" at The John Golden Theater. It had received great reviews. The theater had been the location for the film *A Chorus Line* and I had watched Hume Cronin and Jessica Tandy years before in *The Gin Game*.

Dad was excited to see FJC, but at the same time, it was noticeable how he was so removed from me that night. He had flown in from a trade show in Vegas and was tired. It seemed like when he visited me when I was in my twenties and early thirties, it was exhausting to see me, like a chore. Since we talked on the phone, but had no in person contact except for holidays, I found it very uncomfortable. It was such a difference from my adolescence and teen years with him in Michigan. His little girl was all grown up and hadn't joined him in his businesses. I had basically turned my back on the corporate executive life he had wished for me.

We watched the show quietly. I tried to make conversation, but it was practically impossible. The idea of bringing him back to meet FJC, who probably wouldn't have remembered me anyway, didn't seem like a good idea.

"Great show, honey." Dad was busy pulling out cab money and hailing a taxi, wasting no time getting away from me.

"Dad, um..." I hesitated.

"What is it?" Dad turned as a cab pulled up.

"I know him." I answered.

"You do?" Dad was intrigued. He opened the cab door and we got in.

"Yeah, uh...he's a great comic." I sighed.

"Yes, he is. He's made it...for sure." He nodded. I said nothing. I had work in the morning, and Dad had to fly out to another client in Des Moines. "Thank you, sweetheart, for taking me. We'll go to a diner in the morning for breakfast, ok?" He gave me a quick hug,

"Yup, Dad." I said.

Years later, I was still in New York, but this time as a blonde, living on the Upper West Side of Manhattan. I was divorced and still plugging away on the comedy circuit in between personal training and headshot photography. One night I was coming out of The New York Comedy Club with my buddy, Jimmy, a videographer who was in with The Friars Club and all the comics who hung out there. We'd been friends for years. He was kind of my voice of reality.

"Hey, Lee Lee." The nickname.

"Hey, Jimmy!"

"Guess who's holding court at the Star Diner," he was excited.

"Who?"

"FJC! Come on, let's go to see him."

"You know I met him years ago..." I started to tell him the story.

"He might even remember you," Jim pointed out.

We walked over and from the street, looking through the picture window there he was with six people around his booth, and he was vividly talking. We stepped up to the plate and listened. Jim had videotaped him a month ago at the Friars and I had interviewed a lot of stars in 2005 in a pilot we had for a company called Comedy Express. The channel didn't make it, but I interviewed Soupy Sales, Robert Klein, Mayor Dinkins, Chris Elliot, Abe Vigoda, James Lipton, and The Amazing Kreskin. Point is, we traveled in similar comedy circles so he may have seen us around.

"Hey!" Jim called out and shook his hand.

"Hey there," he finally turned towards me. "Who's the blonde?"

"I'm Leanna. We've actually met before."

"I'd remember you." He was being polite.

"Well, maybe you will. I was with my mom at Sardis and we talked about going into comedy...my Dad and I saw your show..." Figured I spell it out.

He was a blank. "Come on and sit down, you two."

From there we all talked and laughed. In a few minutes he asked for my number. I gave him my card.

"A comic." He read the card.

"Yes. I like to write as well," I added.

"You definitely should write. That's important. I'm looking for someone to write me a movie. I need a new vehicle. I'll call you and we'll talk," he said.

Sure enough a few days later, I got a call.

"Hello, is Leanna there?" the voice was unmistakable.

"This is she." I didn't want to let on I knew exactly who it was.

"Is she the one who writes?" FJC asked.

"Yes, that's me," I said. "Is this..."

"Yes, it's me," he laughed, "and I want to have dinner with you and your mother."

"Oh, that's fantastic." I realized I was mimicking him. It was like FJC, imitating FJC.

"Do you realize you sound exactly like me?"

"I had no idea I'm sounding exactly like you." I laughed.

"You sound exactly like me."

"No way!" We both laughed.

We discussed various topics, especially my out-of-town boyfriend in Florida. "Love, love, love! Everything is special with love...you could think a lamp post was special with love. Oh lamp post, you're fantastic, what a fantastic lamp post, oh it's the greatest thing that's ever happened to me...or that mailbox...OY, what a mailbox...it's blue and it's red and it's got a slider...OY! Well, this is meant to be. Meet me at the diner tonight at seven o'clock." After a great soliloquy on love, FJC was back to business and we set up a meeting.

"Okay," I replied.

Nervously, even though I had been there a thousand times before, I made my way through the starkly lit diner on 8th Avenue. The usual cast of characters were huddled in the booths, a few old men slowly chewing their lox and reading the race report, Midwestern tourists eating the meal like it was the most amazing thing that ever happened to them while garbage was piled high in the street right outside the window, and there, in his booth, was my new mentor in a suit with a American flag in his lapel.

"Hi," I sat down in the diner booth.

"Hello, Leanna. Thanks for coming down." He smiled.

"Oh sure."

"So, you've got to come up with a movie for me. What you got?" he jumped right to it.

"Ah, yes..." This was my first pitch to a celebrity. I was crossing my fingers that out of everything I had over the years that something would hit.

"Well?"

"Okay." So much was spinning in my mind. All my standup buddies knew I was dining with FJC. Some of them were impressed, others weren't. But here I was. Sitting with the comic who was an icon in our culture, and he was asking me for a story.

Nervously, I pitched the first idea. It was about the life of a young standup comic, based on my life, with a father who didn't approve. When the father dies he haunts FJC into helping me—I mean, the comic and they write a successful sitcom together to great acclaim.

A few seconds of dead air...

"Terrible." His expression was stoic.

"What?" Did my brilliance just get dashed in a nanosecond?

"Terrible. If you were in my office right now, I would have told you to get out. That was horrible, the worst idea I've ever heard. That was terrible. No, I don't like that idea. What else you got?"

"Uh..." I was totally shocked. Hello, harsh show business.

"Come on, Miss Nine Million Movie Ideas! I know you can come up with something else." He stared right at me, waiting.

"Okay…" I did have something else, which I didn't think I would need to pitch. It was about FJC as a Rabbi and his twin brother who was an Israeli general. They switch places and total pandemonium ensues. I laid out the entire treatment.

"Now that's more like it" He sat back and nodded.

I was so relieved coffee spilled out of my nose with a breath. "Oh, thank God," I must have said aloud.

"No, thank me. I'll look at this tonight," he affirmed. We talked for a while longer about relationships, comedy, and love. "How is your dad?" an out-of-the-blue question shot out from FJC.

He remembered me talking about my Dad? Not likely. "He passed away in 1998," I stated.

"It happens to everyone. How did he like my show?" he asked.

"Loved it," I smiled. He did.

FJC diverted his attention to a few fans coming up to greet him, then stood up, paid the check, and turned around in his distinctive manner and nodded. "Good job. Let's talk next week." He waved, then pushed his way out the glass door of the diner and onto the damp New York street.

I sat back in the booth, smiling, holding my treatment.-

Flash forward to writing this book, the year 2016. For whatever reason, I did not deliver said treatment to FJC, but I still had the number he gave me back in 2009. Life's short, right? Aw, what the heck: [ring, ring]

*"Hello, you've reached the voicemail of The Ultimate Jew. My award winning show Ready to Rumble is heading to the U.K. this summer, so go online and get your tickets there. What, do I have to do everything for you? What am I, your personal night-on-the-town coordinator? Do I have to call you a date, too? I don't work for Uber, the post office or Ticketron, so you better forget it. Leave your message after the beep. What, like you don't know how to do that…?" (beep)*

"Hey, it's Leanna from the diner...in 2009...Uh, I have your treatment ready!"

I'm still waiting for his call, but in the meantime I did go online to get my show DVD and "Schmucks" poster.

Don't tell him, but I'm still making a few tweaks to that treatment. I'm sure he'll understand.

# Chapter 22: Face Off

*Remember, reporters won't attack what smells good!*

Janet is no stranger to the White House, Royal Family, or major newsroom—whether it be warning Margaret Thatcher against heading into the Falklands or phoning Steve Forbes to urge him to get dermabrasion. Janet's called every major political figure and then some, and even gets a call back or two.

The only way I can say it, is that Janet has a firsthand connection with practically every famous person in the universe. They may not realize it, however, but Janet feels perfectly at home calling our esteemed leaders like Presidents Nixon, Carter, and Bush (forty-one and forty-three). She even dialed famous artist Georgia O'Keefe one week before she passed to tell her how fabulous she was. More mysterious than her floating skull or mystic vaginal folds of orchids, was how Janet found her. To this day, I have no idea, but I think that she actually, after a couple of Martinis, spoke to her personal secretary who then asked that she not call back. Can you imagine Georgia O'Keefe in her last days on Earth wondering who in the hell Janet from Detroit, Michigan, was?

And we're not just talking heads of state and celebs. Major news organizations like CNN, CNBC, MSNBC, and every cable channel she could find would get a scolding from our Diva every night during the '91 Gulf War for giving away "war secrets." Janet has always been "a passionate patriot." Plus, it was a great way of schmoozing to possibly get a TV job for her daughter.

"You're telling the terrorists exactly where our boys are, you idiots!"

she'd shout in the receiver, reprimanding anyone unlucky enough to sit on the news desk that night, "and...I have a gorgeous daughter who's marvelous on camera. What's available, say, in prime time?"

Her first hit, or rub with fame, all started when I was attended the University of Michigan in the 1980's. Russians were evil and Bin Laden was a "mercenary." Everyone wore Topsiders, a rat-tail, Ralph Lauren Polo cologne, a down vest, Cyndi Lauper-inspired earrings, and had a cassette single (cassingle!) of "Changes" by David Bowie. You have to understand this was a very pre-9/11 society that, even with the use of atomic weapons, thought our borders were impenetrable and the British would certainly never darken our doorstep again. In sum, we wore shoulder pads (which somehow made us feel invincible) and every movie chase scene and commercial on the air pulsed with an odd synthesizer refrain.

It was about this time that possibly the stupidest war in history was brewing in the Falklands. Something about "the British are coming" except to a different island, or so Janet thought. In actuality, Argentina—not the scariest of nations—had invaded the Falklands, which had a resident British population. Honestly, the only change would be they would eat more meat. Unfortunately, 655 Argentinian troops died to 255 British, which I still think was sadly quite avoidable. Well, whatever the hullabaloo was all about, Janet was not having it! So after having her morning enema, she got on the horn to England and called the iron lady herself, Margaret Thatcher.

"Hello, give me Parliament," Janet insisted. She had finally gotten 10 Downing Street on the phone. To this day, I have NO idea how she did that.

"Excuse me?" a young Brit questioned.

"You know, where the British hold their meetings...Cheerio!" She laughed. "Did you think Twiggy had a good look? I think she was deathly thin...I was a model too, you know, here in the States, I—"

"Ma'am?"

"And teeth have never been a priority for your people, have they? Anyway, I must speak to Margaret Thatcher, immediately!"

After hanging in there and taking to about fifteen people, my mother finally managed to get the vice secretary of the British Parliament. Again, don't ask.

"Hello, Department of—""

"I just have to say, Dickie," Janet cut her off, "It's none of our business to invade the Falklands without so much as an outfit planned! It's so gauche! You don't need to send Prince Charles and all those boys. Just pay for the island!" Her voice projected strongly.

"Mrs...."

"Conley, darling. I'm from America, your former province." Janet stated matter-of-factly, "Some of us are British, however. Don't let that get out."

"Conley, I'll definitely let Mrs. Thatcher know your concerns."

"Have her call me back on the telly, collect, as soon as possible!" Janet got it in just before the call went to a dial tone.

While Ann Arbor is only an hour or so away from Detroit, that not-so-easily-driven-by-Janet distance allowed me a true opportunity to "find myself" as a young adult. And sophomore year it got even better. I lived on campus in a studio at one of the oldest and most conservative women's dorms at The University of Michigan, Helen Newberry House on Main Street. My room was situated at the end of the third floor hallway facing the road, my window stepping out directly to the roof and a great view. It was also the party corridor. Like a '60s Volkswagen, my little apartment would hold an entire frat or sorority that always eventually flooded outside. I'd get knocks at 3:00 a.m. from the Space Cadets or basically anyone who needed a beer and to chill "up high." Sleep was just an elective in college, apparently, and to make good use of my party status, the dorm elected me as social co-chairwoman, a job I took very seriously.

My best friend Beth was my co-chair and, in raincoats (surprisingly), fedora hats and shades, we called on every dorm and frat on campus standing stoically, stating a la *The Blues Brothers*, "We want to party with you." Then we would hand out our flyer and, kind of like my cheerleading days, abruptly turn and leave. It seemed to be just enough. We had a record 223 parties in a school calendar year of 275 days. After all, growing up I had learned how to throw parties from one of the best. By the way, that was also the year we had a kegger party on the roof and, with the help of Sigma Chi next door, hoisted a quadriplegic up the side of the building to enjoy the festivities. I mean, it was a dorm of mostly nurses and we were smack in the middle of town. Who better to party with? We were very inclusive, as in whoever could make it to the roof, was golden.

The invasion night, all the girls in my dorm, or "newbies" as we were called, gathered in the Great Room downstairs avidly watching the Falklands crisis on the communal television, wondering if this was a *Telemundo* drama or an episode of *Doctor Who* (um, it was on then, wasn't it?). Just then Ann, our Resident Advisor, interrupted the gathering.

"Leanna, your Mom's on the phone, says it's an emergency."

Like this is new.

I headed up to grab my phone. "Mom?" I could already tell she was excited.

"You won't believe it. Guess who's calling me back!"

"Cecil B. De Mille?" I asked.

"Margaret Thatcher!" she announced.

"WHAT?" I dropped my jaw. "She was just on the news!"

"She's calling me back tomorrow!" Janet couldn't contain herself. If jumping is a sound, I think I heard it.

I yelled, "Oh my god, Margaret Thatcher is calling my mom back!" Beth and my other sidekick, Peggy, heard me from down the hall and rushed to learn more about the big news.

Mom began to relay the life-changing story to me. Apparently, she was watching the news, trying to get a hold of Walter Cronkite to get me an internship, and she got a call.

Janet's picked up the phone and a British female voice filled the receiver.

"Hello, Dear, I heard you called about the Falklands."

She just about dropped the receiver. All these years of harassing political officials and newsrooms finally paid off. She might even be able to save some young men's lives. She was on cloud nine.

"Mrs. Thatcher! I'm honored you called!"

"Yes, this is…Janet?" she asked.

"Yes! Thank you so much for calling me back. I know how busy you are."

"Oh, only a few meetings…really," she admitted.

"Oh?" Janet felt extra special. Her self-esteem shot up ten points.

"Yes, well my dear, you see, we have British citizens trapped on the island, and I'm not sure Argentina would just serve them a Chiaroscuro white, you know?" She laughed.

"Right." British humor, Janet guessed.

"I have to send our boys in," the lady stated.

"Isn't there another way, Mrs. Thatcher, to get the citizens out until this cools off? So many boys would die for, I'm sorry, what I think is nothing. We don't want that, do we? Have we not learned anything from history? Just pay Argentina for the island and keep Prince Charles out of it. You don't have to send Charles!" Charles may not have been the best-looking royal, but he was a prince and quite snazzy in blue. "And," at the last minute, she added, "get out of Ireland while you're at it!"

Silence.

"War is the last. But it's our only. And it's my decision about that, and Ireland, too. Thank you and cheerio, dear." The lady hung up.

Thrilled by the call, Mom got a new outfit, had the house cleaned top to bottom, and got the shrubs trimmed up. Then she waited for the press to show up and possibly for Reagan to call her! Even our good friend, a harpist of the Detroit Symphony, told all 235 members that Margaret Thatcher had called Janet.

And back in Ann Arbor, I was the talk of Newberry. Everyone made it a sensation! The details were posted on the bulletin board in the library, in the newsletter, and even the Phi Delta '70s-themed party flier had a picture of Margaret Thatcher doing a Jell-O shot to commemorate the event. "We've got to invite her," we all concluded, since we were on her social radar, apparently. We even remarked to ourselves how Helen Newberry herself, from the antiquated portrait on the entrance wall, looked just like Maggie—well, at least her torso did.

Little did we all know, in a faraway mountain range in Kentucky, in a house on a hill, Andy, a very talented musician and son of Laura, Janet's sister, had walked into the house at 1:00 a.m. He put down his backpack on top of a mountain of paper and turned the kitchen light on. The table was littered with notes.

He read a few: "Hello, Mrs. Conley, I heard you called..." script and "Falkland Islands, population and war statistics..." He couldn't believe it. He ran upstairs, and gently shook Laura awake...

"Mom! Did you talk to Margaret Thatcher tonight?"

Flash forward to 1996. The Presidential Election. We're officially out of the '80s. *Forbes Magazine* CEO and namesake, Steve Forbes, is on the ticket. He had the right philosophy—cater-to-the-rich, big business, more nukes, great cover stories—but he also had one thing Janet couldn't get past, dermatology issues.

Politically speaking, Janet is registered Republican who to this day still professes her love for John F. Kennedy. I'm sure she secretly thought about an illicit presidential affair, like every '60s American housewife. So as shallow as it may sound, if a candidate is not handsome, he's definitely not getting *her* vote. She is constantly on the lookout for an attractive Republican, the perfect political storm, in her mind. (Mr. Mitt Romney, Janet says hello!)

One fine morning when I was home from college, out of the not-so-academic bubble and into reality, I heard Mom exclaiming.

"I can't stand it any longer; he'll lose the primaries if I don't act fast!" Janet grabbed the phone. Sure enough, super sleuth Janet spent an hour finally tracking down the campaign central headquarters and got Forbes' right-hand person on the phone. Oh, if only Janet's super powers were used for the real greater good, we'd have peace in the Middle East and a balanced budget.

"This is the Office of Steve Forbes. How can we help you?"

"I don't need the help," quipped Janet.

"Who is calling?"

"It's Janet!" she practically shouted, enthusiastic about what was to come.

"Ok...Janet."

"Janet Lee Conley, darling, I need to speak to Steve's wardrobe person right away."

"I am not sure he has a wardrobe person, but I can get you his secretary," she reluctantly admitted.

"That will do, thank you." Janet was on a roll.

"Hold on one moment." About ten minutes passed.

"This is Bart Russell," a young man's voice answered.

"Hello, darling," Janet was instantly perked up.

"Uh, hello."

"Bart, I need to speak to Steve immediately."

"Steve Forbes?"

"That's who's running, Bart! You don't know your own candidate?" she said, shocked.

"Ma'am...I...um...let me turn you over to Kathy, his campaign manager."

Another wait, and a new person, a woman, got on the phone.

"I have some wonderful ideas and I want Steve to win. He needs to join the times, he needs to look a lot better. You know how Americans like good-looking men. His clothes are still college days. Instead of a crumpled blue oxford, he needs a starched white collared shirt, beautiful tie, and a well-fitting suit. And tell him to throw out the polyester. White, lightly starched shirts. He can keep the blue blazers, and what's with that old watchband? Does he wear good cologne? Reporters won't attack what smells good."

"Well, I—""

"He needs glasses that fit the shape of his face and are less visible. And," Janet continued, "you must get Steve into a dermatologist to get dermabrasion before the next debate or he'll literally fall on his face. Don't just sit there, get on it! It's not like he doesn't have the money. We have one week and he'll need at least three days to heal from that kind of treatment!"

"Oh, I can't tell him all that," she practically gasped over the phone.

Well, said Janet, "Give him to me and I'll tell him. Put him on. If we tell him, it will make a world of difference. Listen, I know what American women like, believe me, if you have him do these things he will get umpteen more votes. It's worth your taking a chance, so please, Katie," Janet pleaded.

"Kathy…"

"Katie, darling, take a chance. Tell him Janet called and wanted to do these things for your campaign." Janet made her final point.

"Well, I will do it."

"You'll be glad you did and so will he! Good-bye," said Janet.

The campaign manager very nicely took all of Janet's suggestions. I was overhearing the entire conversation. I sat back in my chair, laughing, used to this routine, but as always a bit embarrassed for Janet and for her prey. Who knows, maybe I'd write for *Forbes* one day and the interviewer would be like, "Oh, Conley…oh, that sounds familiar…are you related to that woman who called about Steve's acne…a Janet? Well, thanks for coming in, Leanna…"

So on that fateful Republican debate day, to my utter amazement, we see a slightly red-faced, but smoother skinned, Steve Forbes. Smiling from ear to ear, crisp white shirt, expensive blue blazer, a kicking new watch, and well-fitted glasses. He looked like a million bucks and he even made a few good debate points. When you look and feel good, anything is possible, as Janet would say.

When he lost, Janet was only slightly upset. "Darling, he did win. He's now fashionable for the rest of his life. If only someone else I know took criticism so well. Imagine the things she could accomplish!"

"Thanks a lot, Mom."

"Don't mention it," she shot back.

As Janet returned to eyeing herself in the mirror, I realized how she might have a point. I was so used to tuning her out that I often didn't notice how much other people took her advice and benefited from it. I could tell that reaching out to others and offering her almost-always-unsolicited opinion was her way of trying to help, to make a difference. And with the way she carried herself, and with her marginal amount of notoriety, people often took her seriously. Her delivery and her message was always so passionate and direct and well-mannered that many assumed she must know what she's talking about.

And I certainly couldn't deny her chutzpa to say whatever she thought to anyone within earshot—whether it was the media, the royalty family or a would-be President of the United States.

There have been many times when I've wished that I had just an ounce of her assertiveness and confidence. Sometimes on a job interview or dealing with a rude customer service rep or standing on stage in front of a tentative crowd, I will think about how Janet would handle the situation. It helps me put things into perspective and gives me a morale boost.

*Of course you should hire me, I'm perfect for the role!*

*You will refund my balance and give me a free year of cable, won't you, darling?*

*If you want to hear the punch line, you'll have to stop talking amongst yourselves, thanks so much!*

No matter what situation I'm in, a daily dose of Janet usually does the trick.

# Chapter 23: Miracle Roots

*Regrets are for the lazy and unfashionable!*

In 2010, it had been over forty-five years since the miracle of my birth took place and as you can image, Janet and I had made our way through a myriad of experiences included many emotional ups and downs. However, despite the dramatics, the emotions, and the tricky dynamics of most any mother/daughter relationship, Janet managed to surprise even me when she matter-of-factly shared her feelings about what I had only assumed was one of the best experiences of her life... my birth.

There is much societal pressure in a woman's life to have children while she can. That pressure rudely interrupted Janet's booming modeling career. I haven't had any children; I'm past that now. While in many ways I regret this, I'm actually glad things have turned out that way. I love kids and I'd rather hang out with children than adults a majority of the time, but the true rigors of parenthood, quite frankly, terrify me.

Some people have even told me that, quite candidly, it's selfish if you don't have a child. Well, I think you're selfish if you can't handle a child and you have one. Believe me, that is much worse. To that point, Janet did the best that she could, and I know she loves me more than her own life. That said, she has been, in my mind, a woman who never should've had a child. Her energy for stardom, this zeal for life, could and did turn into depression, darkness, and a terrible ugliness when her dreams went unfulfilled. She now lives vicariously through me, which can't be healthy for either of us.

"I wish you were never born." It was an average New York City night during a "normal" phone conversation when Janet made that matter-of-fact statement. I was in my forties and recently divorced. Stunned by its ultimate bluntness, it was like a verbal *hara-kiri* knife twisting in my self-esteem.

I asked her again, "Do you realize what you're saying?"

"Of course I do! I should have had an abortion…" she said, nonchalantly as if ordering a duvet cover from Neiman Marcus or reading the Style page. She shared other bits of information about problems she thought I needed to fix, they ranged from my life in general to my boyfriends, my looks; it just went on and on. I really began to wonder if her mother had done that to her. Maybe it was some sort of warped tradition.

She did tell me once that her mother criticized her, but I don't think on the level that I received. Belle Bailey Conley, my grandmother, was a businesswoman to the nth degree. She was a leader and a force to be reckoned with. My father even drew up plans for her hotel and restaurant, which she began at seventy-two and ran well into her eighties. If ever there was a role model for my mother, it was Belle B. Janet would have done well to follow Belle's lead: Never a sad sack day in her life, always a fighter, and above all a realist. She eventually had nine children in total, a huge responsibility she bore well, in addition to her businesses.

Unbeknownst to me until now, however, Belle did have an infatuation in her teens with, of all unpractical things, being a star. She had packed her trunk in 1920, ten years before Mom popped out into the Kentucky wilderness, and headed to Florida of all places. Apparently things didn't work out because she ended up back home in Kentucky. And that, my friends, is all I know about Belle's run-in with stardom. She quickly settled into being a realist, married my grandfather Warren Conley that weekend after she came home, and started what in those days was inevitable, working as a teacher in a one-room schoolhouse, and of course, having babies. With birth control being limited to a Bible on the nightstand, that was the way the pregnancy cookie crumbled. And it's no mistake that by her ninth child we can document she never smiled in pictures. Frankly, I couldn't blame her. It would seem her young dreams ended up as the role of a mother with nine kids she couldn't tame, with Janet playing the lead in that real-life play.

But in a way, Janet did "work" at her imaginary realm. She didn't want to fare the climb to glory or defeat herself. That was a battle for her daughter to fight. For Janet, as a young woman, and now as an elder, there was only one thing in her way and that was fear.

I finally got through to her how hurtful that comment was to me. Realizing its depth and devastation, she was so hell-bent on showing me how much she loved me that she decided to drive me to my birthplace one time when we went back to visit friends in Detroit. I'm not talking about the hospital. I'm talking about the Red Run Apartments in Royal Oak, Michigan, where I was conceived sometime in November 1961 (ten months back from my birthday, August, 31, 1962).

After a short drive down Woodward Avenue, we pulled into the Red Run Apartments and stopped right in front of unit 109, a hunter-green door in a modest, unassuming building with basic shrubs and utilitarian cars adorning the exterior.

"Mom, seriously…" I gave her a frowning look.

"Leanna, this is where you were not only conceived, but planned. Of course I had imagined you with bigger breasts as an adult, but you can always have those implanted, darling. Other than that, you're my masterpiece," she exclaimed.

We knocked on the door. A middle-aged woman in a housedress answered.

"Hello…" Janet said in a sweet voice. She had a beautiful caped coat and brown kit boots, gloves and gorgeous leather bag. I wasn't so bad myself, rocking jeans, boots, and a Fendi black down jacket with fur hood.

"Hello?" The woman cocked her head trying to place Janet. "What are you selling?"

"Oh, not selling, darling." Janet calmed her down. "My husband and I used to live here."

"Last year? Our sink leaks and we have termites," Betsy said matter-of-factly.

"No, darling, in 1962." Janet smiled.

"Oh." She was now clueless. Betsy stared at me. I shrugged.

"I'm Janet and this is my amazing daughter, Leanna/"

I awkwardly smiled.

"And you are…"

"I'm Betsy. This isn't *Publisher's Clearinghouse?*"

"Betsy, darling! Just two seconds of your time." Janet greeted her as if they were old friends and walked right past her blocking maneuver and into the foyer. I timidly followed. "My, is that Chanel Crystal you're wearing, Betsy?" For some reason, the lady let us in.

"Well…" She processed that for a second, nodded her head and realized indeed, it was a compliment.

"Hmm, nice setup here," said Janet, surveying the kitchen and living room. "You see, my daughter was conceived somewhere around here…" She started her story and quickly got down to brass tacks.

"I need to see the corner of your upstairs bedroom, Betsy. It's an emergency," Janet insisted. The downstairs was basically a brown motif. Very '70s with a beige corduroy sofa, shag carpet, sparse walls, and a flat screen television with a lone plant by its side. It was very utilitarian.

"You could do with a bit of redecorating, Betsy. This place was immaculate forty years ago. Dump those cheap chairs over there, and you call those curtains?" Janet scolded.

Betsy covered her hand to her mouth, a bit ashamed.

"My husband Bill and I were here in 1960 and we only made twenty bucks a week so get cracking, darling. Money is no excuse! *Better Homes and Gardens* should be online by now…"

Betsy nodded. "Okay, uh, Janet, is it?"

We made our way upstairs to the master bedroom. Mom pointed to the far corner. It was sparse with again, the drab motif continued: a brown dresser, checkered wallpaper with a picture of Jesus hanging crookedly on one of the walls.

"Eureka! That was the spot!" She was in awe, she almost sang the words.

"Okay…" I nodded.

"Honey," she turned to me, "this is where I stood on my head after intercourse with your father to make sure that strong little spermatozoa got to the egg."

"In that corner?" Betsy said, seeming slightly dazed by the very vivid information. "Under the picture of…?" Betsy gasped.

"So you see, Sweetheart, you *were* planned. And I wasn't leaving anything to chance!" she announced proudly. She hugged me, her cold kid leather gloves squeezing my coat with fervor.

"Well, um, thanks, Mom?" Actually I was genuinely moved, but also stunned and a bit embarrassed that we had overrun poor Betsy's apartment.

"Don't worry, dear Betsy, that was quite some time ago. I mean, see exhibit A," she said, pointing at me.

If Janet could have gotten sperm samples from decades ago to prove her point I think she would have, as she examined the corner like an investigator on *CSI: Special Victims Unit.*

"Look at the result of all that hard work! Amazing stuff! Don't you agree?" Janet smiled.

"Good Lord, Mom…" I said starting to laugh myself silly.

"Yes," said Betsy, "my husband and I are also very fortunate. One is on the way." Betsy seemed pretty inspired herself.

"Congratulations!" Janet clapped her hands together. "Start playing Puccini and wear a skirt. Leanna sang Italian at age three and even speaks French. Say something for her, darling."

"*Oui.*" I nodded.

"Thanks for the tips, Janet!"

"Ok, Mom," I said pulling her sleeve, "I think we're good here."

"Well, thanks again, Betsy, and remember if you want an outstanding child, you know where you can do it!" Janet pointed to the corner as I waved good-bye.

It was a quiet car ride to Saks Fifth Avenue in Birmingham, Michigan, along the Woodward Avenue corridor. We did our usual shop-and-lunch scenario, buying clothes I didn't always care for, but then I'd find myself appreciating them later. I liked the compliments I received after modeling a wardrobe from a recent shopping spree, and heeded my mother's words about the formidable weapon called appearance.

These extremes sum up this roller-coaster life I've lived with Janet. She could devastate me with a comment like saying I wasn't really wanted and then go out of her way to prove that I was actually carefully planned. It was that dichotomy that often drives me crazy, but on the other hand, helps me to understand my mother and see her as a very real, very complex woman. I realized that her flair for the dramatics and her often caustic statements were just her way of dealing with her tragedies and the sometimes daunting task of forgetting them.

Like most of us, I think things didn't turn out quite as Janet had planned, but I also think that she slowly realized that maybe that's the way life works. If we could all plan out exactly how things will unfold, what would be the point of living it? The joy is in the journey, the not knowing. Life is about the surprises that we experience along the way.

And surprises are Janet's specialty.

# Chapter 24: Knockers Up!

*Anyone can be practical, not everyone can be fabulous!*

"I can't get my damn window to roll up!" Janet, dressed in those Hugh Heffner-esque PJs and curlers, revs the engine of her Cadillac for the entire retiree neighborhood to hear. Honking and swearing, she puts the pedal to the metal—all while the car is in park. She's on her fifth Caddy.

It is a hot, muggy Saturday night in the Florida Panhandle and we are back at Janet's townhouse at Lionsgate. I am waiting on my first date arranged through Plenty of Fish (POF), an online dating service. I can only hope he looks something like his picture. After living in New York City for most of my adult life, I had moved to Florida in 2009 just in time for the BP oil spill. So, here I am, fifty and single in an economically depressed area with a long line of rejected "Florida boyfriends" since my breakup and divorce a few years earlier. By the way, the grass isn't always greener...

"Janet! Stop hitting the gas!" I plead. I point out the "Up" button on the driver's door. I had hoped to get Janet out of the car and back in the house before the big date, but I knew better. "That's the button. Push it!" I thank the Lord she didn't shift gears. Janet has finally figured out how to operate the electric window and gas pedal simultaneously. She is ready! (For what, I'm not sure.)

"Let's roll!" She blows the horn for emphasis.

"Where?" I ask in a panic.

"To get cigarettes!" Janet exclaims.

I remember the last time she embarked on getting cigarettes. We almost plowed over a blind guy in the parking lot of the Circle K. And yes, I admit it, she actually shouted at him through the open window: "Watch it! What are ya? Blind?"

"Mom, please get inside! My date will be here any minute!" As soon as I utter the word "minute," John, the date, pulls up in his Beemer. I'm in heels and Janet is in her robe and curlers, a mirror image of my exact look an hour before (and will be again in about three hours if this is anything like my other dates).

Not bad for an online match, he is cute with a nice shirt, jeans, nice shoes (very key), and a great smile. I hope my own killer outfit can distract him from the little lady at the wheel swearing and honking.

"Hi, John." I give a half-hearted greeting because terror is seeping out of every one of my pores.

"I'm Janet, dammit." She waves and gives him a wink. She's vamping even in curlers.

I hold my breath. "Mom, John. John, Janet."

"Hello, Janet. I'm John." He starts to shake her hand.

"Well, hello, darling! My, you're a big one." She isn't staring at his stature.

"Mom," I whisper, "I told you to scram before he picked me up. Now, be nice and go inside."

"Well, it's an emergency! I need cigarettes!" Janet pounds the wheel with her hand to add the needed emphasis. She means it. Cigarettes trump everything, even dates. I can see her now in a frenzy behind the wheel, mopping the highway with more blind men, and taking down a few panhandlers if necessary.

"We can go get some," John offers, giving me a quick, empathetic hug. That made me like him a little bit more. I always love these moments before they have experienced Janet. They seem so innocent.

"I like this guy," says Janet. "Are you a doctor?"

"I'm in sales."

"Shit!" Janet frowns. "Guess it could be worse."

*Okay, this isn't happening,* I think to myself. I am mortified, of course, but not totally. As always, I combine it with laughter to create a feeling of being "lortified"—an emotion I coined soon after the Hot Dog

Lunch fiasco in grade school. Some things you just never forget no matter how hard you try.

"Let's get your mom some cigarettes, Leanna, and then we can go to the Global Grill," John suggests. Poor thing has no idea what he's dealing with.

"I've changed my mind, John. You're all right." Janet jumps out of her car and heads toward his Beemer. She pats him on the back.

John politely opens the back of the coupe for her. "Great," I sigh as we pile into this stranger's car. Mom is in the back crawlspace, facing forward.

"Next time you get a bonus, buy a four-door, not a coupe. You're not twenty-five anymore," Janet scolds.

John helps her fit in the space more comfortably. "Of course," he says.

*Dear Lord,* I think, *what now?* To my surprise, John handles the situation like a seasoned psychiatric social worker.

"Janet, you smell marvelous. What's your perfume?" he asks.

Janet and I both start to say "Chanel" at the same time. We look at each other for a nanosecond, and then laugh. Earlier that day Janet had tried to dress me for my date. She had stockings, open lipsticks, makeup, and a counter filled with different colored lip liners, mirrors, and curlers all ready and waiting on every flat surface in order to ambush me as soon as I got home, pulling out the stops for her little fashion plate.

For my date nights, so hell bent has she been on getting her baby married, she has set out drinks, candles, hors d'oeuvres, and all kinds of amenities to help the cause—in case the dates have come "home." And tonight is no different. Janet has something special prepared for me. She's made me a "salad drawer."

Okay, by that I don't mean she put some individual veggies in the crisper section of the fridge. I mean she turned the crisper drawer in the fridge into a fully functional salad bowl complete with loose lettuce, tomatoes, oil, vinegar, and croutons all tossed together, just swimming around in clear plastic. Earlier in the day, she called my attention to her new creation.

"So," she says, posing by the fridge, "when you have guys over, you can just say, 'Want a salad, honey?'"

She proceeds to open the crisper drawer...eyes wide. "Well, you got it. Tossed and ready!" Waving her tongs, she adds. "Come and get it!"

I snap out of the salad flashback.

Janet starts roaring with laughter from the backseat. "I wish I went on all your dates. Then you wouldn't pick such losers...present company excluded, of course!"

"Mom!" I snap back, quickly looking at John to detect any changes in his expression. *Whew, ok.* He's laughing. John has a sense of humor. *Three points there and thank the Lord.*

"Hey, I'm starving," blurts Janet.

"No, you are not." I smile over my clenched teeth.

"Well, how about McDonald's?" she suggests.

I look at John. "Okay," he acquiesces.

Janet then proceeds to talk in great detail about how she hates every politician but Kennedy. I sink further down into the gray leather. *Please do not talk politics,* I think, *or anything else!*

We get to the drive-thru voice box, and he turns around to face Janet.

"Janet, what would you like?" He's sure got the charm part down.

"A Budweiser!" Janet claps her hands together like a kid a Christmas.

"Mom, this is McDonald's. McDonald's doesn't have beer, or cigarettes I might add!"

"Shit. Well, a coke and a hamburger, well done," she concedes. After waiting for what seemed like a century for Mom's well-done, fast food hamburger, I speak up. "Mom, we've got to get to the restaurant."

We hurry back to drop Janet off. After a few more minutes of conversation, consisting of embarrassing personal nuggets—like I should have married John-John Kennedy and Grace Kelly was a princess just like her daughter should have been—we deliver little Janet safely home, complete with her menthol Virginia Slims, hamburger, Coke, and bridge mix. That should keep her busy for at least a couple of hours.

I look at my mom, now older, frail, and standing in the doorway, a vision I've seen many times. My outrage turns to sympathy and understanding. I hug her.

"Leanna," Mom squeezes me back, "I love you, honey. But this guy's not good enough. You are my life."

"I know, Mom."

"Now go have a good time and don't forget, knockers up!" She sprays me with perfume she has tucked in her robe as if she were macing an intruder. Then, without warning, she kicks up her leg in the air.

"Knockers up, Mom." I kick my leg up in response. "Call me if you need me. And don't smoke in bed or use the stove, okay? And you know where the salad is."

"AHHHH, I'll be all right…but put on more lip liner, please. You're lacking color!" She hands me a compact and red lip liner.

"Okay." I say, as I slip it into my purse.

"And you need a coat!" She runs back into the house. After going through the closet to get five coats out, like she usually does, she brings them to me.

"You know, it is seventy-two degrees…" I reluctantly take the puffy brown coat and throw it over my arm. Mom looks at me, satisfied.

"Bye, Mom!" I turn and bolt toward this stranger's car like my life depends on it. I sit down with a brief sigh and look at my date. John nods toward our front door, "I can tell she really loves you."

He smiles.

*Hmm. I just might invite him in to experience the "salad drawer" tonight after all.*

"Let's start this off again, shall we? I shake his hand once more. "Hi, I'm Leanna. And that …was Janet."

# Epilogue

### Los Angeles, September, 2016

I'm in the Green Room at the Hudson Theater with Amy Schumer and Sarah Silverman. They're my new best friends, wishing me well for my Comedy Central Special. Tonight is the night. There's the lights, the cameras, I step on a large black stage to face my first TV taping in front of a hushed crowd. Shaking, I begin...

"My mother drinks a lot, but that's what 'socialites' do...on her tomb stone, they're putting R.I.P.P.E.D." My first joke kills and the audience is going crazy. Ah! At last, I've arrived. But there's one crazy laugh in the crowd that gets louder and louder...and LOUDER...

"Ha!" Janet is leaning over me with a hair dryer, trying to style my bangs. "Just want a curl before you make your debut tonight!"

I got up from my nap with a start, thinking about the crazy dream I had and then realizing my mother was styling me while I slept. I'm not sure which was more disturbing. When I look at Janet, there's no denying her beauty, even at eighty-three. Her perfectly manicured red nails are still grasping and twisting my hair to perfection since she's determined to get me in the make-me-perfect zone.

I glance in the mirrored wall of her new L.A. pad. Just a few months ago, we hauled our cookies from the golden walls of sunny Pensacola to her new home at the Piedmont Senior Center in Hollywood, California, Janet's forever home. I couldn't not heed the call anymore plus she loves the center's activities, particularly dirty joke night. In her spare time she does makeovers for all the women in the center, and even their pets!

Tonight, she has arranged a special evening for her daughter to do standup for the residents during what would have been "Taco Tuesday." The entertainment committee cautiously agreed since they were still sizing up Janet, their newest member and something of a local celebrity. I hear the residents talking about her in what they think are whispers.

*She used to be a Revlon spokesmodel.*
*I think she turned down Playboy.*
*Oh, I heard she posed for Playboy!*
*She was a stylist for Jimmy Hoffa!*

I put on my nicest suit, the one I've worn for various New York shows, a few TV pilots gone awry, and even job interviews for paralegal work while keeping the dream alive.

"Darling! You look marvelous." Janet hugs me. I smile. Her once critical tone has softened over the years. All she had for me this evening were words of praise, and some mangled but well-intentioned bangs.

"Oh, Brit told me she needs vodka, so we have to run over to Ralph's and score some!"

"Well, I think there's wine, Mom."

"Nonsense! Who can party with wine? These LA lightweights..."

"We have an appointment at Central Casting next week, you know. I have my outfit all planned!"

"I know. I got you an appointment with my manager. And no doubt you will be the hit of the century."

I had already made Janet some beautiful headshots and worked carefully on preparing her resume. I knew she'd be excited just to sit in a casting office for hours, not realizing how really uneventful showbiz actually is. And of course, I wasn't going to spoil it for her.

As we were leaving, I went back to get Mom's purse from the dresser. She was forgetting many things now, and much more frequently. The doctors assured me that it was normal, whatever that means. So now I do most of the caretaking and shopping for her. Last night I brought her an Ensure and you'd think it was the stuff of legends. She raved she was so excited.

These days it really is the little things, and that's okay with both of us. It's truly an honor to take care of the woman who motivated and inspired me, even if I didn't actually achieve everything she had envisioned for her little girl. I think she has come to understand that our dreams may not have been exactly the same, but we embarked on this journey together and we're still enjoying the ride.

Just before we left for the show, I saw her staring out the window, as if dizzy or confused. I put my hand gently on her shoulder and she sprung back to life, as animated as ever.

"I'm ready," she announced as she popped up. "How do I look, honey? That handsome Larry Johnson is going to be there and I don't want him to miss a thing!" She quickly flashed her leopard bra under her black blazer. Some things never change.

"Mom, you look perfect."

That night I killed in the Piedmont Recreation Room to an audience of five people, and I think only two were awake through the entire set. However, none of that mattered. Janet was beaming with pride, her eyes just misty with a trickle of mascara sliding down her cheek.

"Do Kennedy," she shouts loudly, creating a small echo amidst the stacked chairs, white boards and over-used props.

I bring her up on the little makeshift stage and imitate her favorite president while she howls with laughter. We work the crowd, a true duo, she imitating Jacqueline Kennedy Onassis and I, JFK, aka the old Vaughn Meader 1960's comedy albums. We had that entire record down and used to do it at parties for captive audiences.

She loved it. She was entranced. And, in that moment, everything felt right.

It was THE DAILY JANET SHOW...and it always will be.

# Janet's Modeling Book

*May the wind be at your back and Coco Chanel be in your closet!*

As a little girl, I was naturally fascinated by my mother's childhood stories, even if I was never really sure they were 100% legit. Time allows us to reflect and shape our memories, making them more exciting (or less so) by suppressing the things we didn't like. So when I heard from both of my parents the tales of modeling shoots and big contract offers, I was wary but interested. It sounded so glamorous and worldly. And I could see by the way Janet carried herself and interacted with others that some type of training had occurred. I had seen the select photos that adorned our home, but it wasn't until I found a stash of carefully stored mementos that I realized just how determined she had been to follow her dreams.

From 1951-1962, Janet had thrown herself wholeheartedly into what came naturally, modeling. When all was said and done, she had been offered the job of Revlon spokesmodel in 1961, as well as being chosen as a *Playboy* centerfold. Since they were in Detroit, her main modeling clients were auto shows for Ford and General Motors (and since she had a Caddy, and always has, she felt right at home at GM).

The only training she had was as a student at The Patricia Stevens Modeling School in Cincinnati, for a whopping day and a half. On the second day, a representative from Warner Bras walked into the class and wanted to know if anyone there was a 34C bra size and naturally Janet spoke up. "I am! I'll do it, what is it?" With that, her modeling career was born. So at the Brown Hotel in Louisville, Kentucky, she had her first catwalk. She even bounced a ball while walking up on the stage, which was a bit more activity than the other girls. In those days, even though they were modeling bras, the girls couldn't get fully naked so they put full-floor length "tulle" skirts on all the models.

Next, she had her composite photos, where a photographer puts together various shots to show the model's range. Hers were taken in Detroit on the rooftops of a few buildings. There was one with a sun hat and a scarf around her head, hair wet, and sparse makeup, then posed behind an iron wheel, which she thought would be a fitting look for the Motor City!

It turned out the composites worked even better than she had planned. Her best shot was in a pink sheer bodysuit; pink tights and heels that were so sexy her photographer advised her not to use it. "You'll get the wrong kind of calls," he warned.

Janet was as happy as a clam being an in-demand model going on various shoots all over the city until one day, Dorothy Siebert, the biggest agent in Detroit at the time, called. "Janet, you better be sitting down. They want you to be the TV spokesmodel for a large cosmetic company! You have the job if you want it. You don't even have to audition. The guy knows your work and he wants you and you only."

Janet was twenty-seven, living with my dad, Bill, and they were considering having a child (uh, you know who). If she took the job as spokesmodel for the company that turned out to be Revlon, it would require that she leave Detroit and live in New York or Los Angeles, away from the comfortable life she shared with her husband. Would he support her in this? Would she ever have a family? If she did say yes, this could be everything she ever dreamed.

She told Dorothy, "I'll think it over."

Dad seemed neither encouraging nor upset when she told him the news that night. He said, "You decide." There wasn't more to it, really.

Janet called Dorothy the next morning to turn her down.

"What?" said Dorothy, "Are you crazy? You've got the chance of a lifetime. You've hit the jackpot. Girls would kill for this!"

"Dorothy, I think I'll have a baby instead." While the good news (for me) was that I would be born, I found out that in reality, Janet was scared and a baby gave her a way out. She didn't know if she was good enough and she was terrified of failure. She'd had a small taste of it in school and didn't like it one bit. She was afraid she wouldn't be perfect. Turning down Revlon is a decision she's never forgiven herself for (and I was unintentionally blamed as well). She regrets her seemly poor choice: She could have had it all (except without me). You would think with her moxie and determination it would have been a natural option. If she had only possessed the confidence and self-assurance that she projected onto the world, things could have turned out very differently. As is often the case, she was riddled with self-doubt on the inside, not seeing the potential that others saw, and most importantly afraid of losing the stability she had always craved.

"I didn't think about it long enough to weigh the pros and cons properly. I could have had a baby two or three years later," Mom confessed.

"Mom, then it wouldn't be me!" I pointed out a bit disappointed.

"Well of course, you would have just been a couple years younger..." she reasoned. "And who wouldn't want that, darling?"

And then there was another missed opportunity, *Playboy*. Hugh Heffner was opening his new Playboy Club in Detroit. Janet and many other girls from her agency went to visit the club they had heard so much about. Hugh came over to their table immediately, sat next to Janet, and asked if she wanted to be a bunny. "I'm not going around with a cotton ball on my tail!" she retorted. He patted one of the other girls on the butt as she turned to go to the power room. "What a letch!" she later reported to Bill. Back then, the Hef wasn't such a fatherly figure, as he's portrayed today.

After a few days had passed, a photographer from *Playboy* grabbed Janet from the catwalk of a fashion show she was working. "Oh, dear, you have the bone structure of Suzy Parker!" (Suzy was THE model of the 1960s.) "Will you do our centerfold?"

"Naked?" Mom said.

"Just the top," he assured her.

"Well, yes."

Mom said she wasn't nervous about that one. "I knew my breasts were perky and my body was beautiful...and thank goodness they didn't show your vagina like they do now! Can you just imagine?" It wasn't something I really wanted to think too much about.

Mom told Dad about the job after her fashion show that day. The pay was $500 and a fur coat! Not bad for back then. Dad had been very supportive of her work so far, but this was just too much for him. He thought about the guys at work and how others might react. To him the risk just wasn't worth the reward. Janet reluctantly agreed with him, but secretly she wondered how things may have changed if for once she had said "yes."

## Cincinnati test shoot – The Beginning

Janet started her modeling career with this shot. The photographer's friend snapped this picture of Janet's pose. Great concept. After this session, they encouraged her to "do it full time!" She was a blonde. Later, she'd model as a redhead to stand out as most of her competitors were blondes or brunettes.

## Mommy Mermaid and Other Themed Shows

Mom was a mermaid for a "fantasy hair show" in the late '50s. While many jobs were modeling clothes, modeling "hair" was also a popular '50s and '60s fad. I mean, you had groovy Matt Helm movies with spy chicks in go-go boots and of course James Bond babes…concept shows were lauded. Lovely Mermaid Janet was complete with skintight body suit and tail! The costume was so tight she couldn't walk, not to mention dealing with the tail, so her hairdresser and a few other stylists carried her on the stage. And, she even won a certificate from the Governor of Michigan for "best model." Not quite sure if that was for her hair or for just being amphibious!

## Janet as Goddess Pele

Mom did a similar hair show at the Statler's Ballroom in Detroit where she was the awesome Goddess Pelé, Hawaiian Goddess of the Volcano. The runway went all around the audience of buyers, department store owners, businessmen, and women and then circled up to the middle of the audience "like a stripper's stage!" The picture shows her being worked on by her hairdresser, Eddie. The headdress was gold; she wore gold lame pants and gold lame strapless top, gold heels. She worked a long, gold floor-length cape and that wasn't all. She had a parrot companion named Pretty Boy on her left arm resting on a bird of paradise flower armband. "And that little son of a bitch and I would talk! He laughed exactly like me! Anywhere I was in the room he'd fly to me when he heard me. We put on a show for the audience like crazy. We sang and brought the house down—'Anything You Can Do I Can Do Better'…and I made him talk to the emcee. He did anything

I asked him. He liked me, well, he liked my Martinis!"

She added that she unabashedly shared her drink with him (not recommended by the World Wildlife Federation by the way). Pretty Boy stayed with Janet the night before the show. "He was so mean, nobody else could handle him. And before the show, to calm him down, I gave him two or three sips of my Martini! It was magic!"

## Mom and Dad Hosted Award Night for Theaters in the Detroit Area

The cute couple emceed the event in the voices of Ronald Coleman and Katharine Hepburn. "That went over big, naturally, with the theatre group. We could do no wrong, anyway!" Janet said. That's the night when Janet got "Best Supporting Actress in the Detroit Area" for her performance in the play *You Can't Take It With You!* "Dad looked so handsome in his tux!" exclaimed Mom. Dad used to coach Mom's speaking voice like Rex Harrison to her Eliza Doolittle to rid her of the Kentucky twang. The guy accepting the award was their dear friend Conrad, the other clean-cut guy was a local actor. I don't have a photo of Dad in his tux, unfortunately. But he was always Rod Taylor/Tyrone Power handsome! Here's a shot of Janet being *film noire*

mysterious before the award party.

Janet on top of actor, Uncle Chester on the side falling,
in the play *You Can't Take It With You!*

Janet won an award for Best Supporting Actress for her performance in *You Can't Take It With You*. She played the role of an alcoholic full of surprises. During the play she was asleep on stage under an afghan. Halfway through, she jumped up from her inebriated slumber to do her monologue and the afghan, which was accidentally pinned to her dress, was caught. Thinking quickly, she pulled the pin and ripped off the afghan, singing, "Put the blame on Mame, boys, put the blame on Mame!" Even with a wardrobe malfunction, Janet did her stuff, and the show did go on. The crowd laughed and applauded. She was so proud that she was the only one to get an ovation. After her dance, she turned to go upstairs, tripped and fell on her costar's lap (see photo) and the chair broke. They both hit the floor and got *another* big laugh from the audience. My Uncle Chester helped her up and she staggered up the steps, which were really precarious…they had accidentally broke the chair in rehearsal, but it got such a laugh from the crowd they kept it in every performance. Not sure how they fixed the chairs to break like it did, but that's the magic of show business! The next photo, Janet and Chester were up to their old tricks at the after-party when they were dancing.

The group was on a retreat up north in Michigan at a cabin and they partied all night long. That night they captured Janet in various poses and eventually here she is caught collapsing on Chester after attempting to lift him up, and that's when she sprained her ankle.

Turns out, I was there, too. Mom was three months pregnant. A few months later, I was ready to be taken along to the parties in my little bassinette, holding down the coatroom. Janet would check on me in-between dances. The entire theater group, I must say, adopted me and, hence, my love of theater.

Not only did I party with the group as a kid, I modeled. Here I am in

Cadillac, Michigan at Saks Fifth Avenue show with an unknown young lady during the kids segment. We're in matching daisy swimsuits (I also modeled with Janet on the runway but didn't find the pictures.) I wasn't as smiley as the lovely Janet, but eventually I got the drill and starting working the runway like a pro. When I was older (8-12), I modeled on my own.

## Cook Out Charcoal Lighter Fluid

*Detroit News* for Cook Out Charcoal Lighter fluid ad. Ran in 1957. Just a typical gorgeous product shot for our Daily Janet, I mean, who wouldn't buy it now?

The next two shots were in the newspaper, her first official Detroit modeling job ran in *The Detroit News* in 1955! Janet modeled a silk Japanese scarf to show the versatile ways to wear them, first as a window dressing and then, standing full body shot behind a beaded curtain with the scarf dressing her! Of course, it was just to show off her amazing figure.

# Janet wardrobe shot in modeling composite

Pink dress, Janet's hands are up. Janet designed the dress and had it made with pink and white polka-dot silk and pretty shoes. Janet's signature back panel really made the dress outstanding. Just one of the many she had in her glorious closet. It's Absolutely Janet!

# Janet black bathing suit full shot in composite

Here we have a one-piece beautiful fitting suit. They decided Janet should wear this suit – the other they had shot was a pink sheer body suit with tiny diamonds and pink stockings with sparkles and high heel shoes.

## Janet with umbrella handle dividing face in composite

On an impulse, Janet posed with an umbrella handle in the middle of her face and the "photogs" loved it, saying: "Janet that's great, let's keep it in."

## Janet sitting in Cadillac in black suit and heels

This is Janet's 1957 Cadillac. Janet had on a designer silk suit with a portrait neckline, which she says is very flattering. Most of her clothes she bought at Giddy's, a very exclusive shop in Detroit, or she designed them and had them made. And, of course they fit like a dream. Janet thought the car interior showed the suit off well and they could light up the car easily. And since it's Motown and you got the best jobs

modeling cars, it was a must for the composite. Mom and Dad had lunch with the Governor of Michigan, George Romney and Mrs. Romney, at The Bloomfield Hills Country Club shortly after Dad had moved up in status as an auto executive. Janet had on this outfit. Dad didn't tell Mom where they were going that night because he felt Janet might be a bit nervous, but she fit right in, darlings! Janet and Bill were a little surprised to notice that they were the only guests attending; the rest were, Janet realized, bodyguards. And I'm sure she impressed them, too. (Hello, Kevin Costner!)

I loved looking at photos of Janet's modeling days, and I'd ask her questions: What was it like to model (which I would later find out on my own gigs). The auto shows she worked in Detroit, Janet says, were not too eventful. "You just stand there on the turntable with the featured car, but it's exhausting. And the spotlight is on the car. They buff it, polish it, they treat it like a baby and when they finally bring it out, I'm exhausted. But in the long run, it's fun. We always had parties afterward, dancing and drinking at the best spots in town. Sometimes Bill would meet us, sometimes not, but I'd tease every guy that came along to the party! And a boom, and a boom, and a boom, boom, boom." Mom had to wait around the set when she did acting, just like the auto show. It's the after party where the real modeling always began!

Janet and Bill at The Palmer House, Chicago, 1958

# Janet's Closet

*It's Absolutely Janet, darling!*

All models have their wardrobe. Janet had designed and made many beautiful clothes, from her teens to adult years. I'd marvel at the exquisite dresses, jewelry, and shoes she had in the closet when I was a child. A girl's dress-up dream! And with each outfit, there's a bit a history and always a "Janet story."

This beautiful outfit was designed by Janet for the lead in the play *The Philadelphia Story*. The flowing back panels and pantsuits were worn by many stars of the day. Her theater group gave her a lot of inspiration and many afterglow parties and an opportunity to hobnob with famous actors!

*A-line silk pink-colored party dress* – This is the infamous *You Can't Take it With You* party dress design. One of her favorite theater group party dresses, this little number was airy, fun, and the skirt would swish as she turned. This is the dress Janet wore the night she sprained her ankle dancing with Uncle Chester. (We love Uncle Chester…who has wild stories of his own!)

*The brown chiffon dress* (also like her pink dress, seated at her wardrobe in her composite. Janet met George C. Scott in this dress at a fundraiser to build a theater in Detroit. "What a fascinating, handsome woman you are!" said George. Janet had turned around in the theater lobby cocktail line and replied, "Well, look who's saying that, hi ya, George, you're pretty handsome yourself!" He and his wife Colleen Dewhurst took tickets at the door for the fundraiser. The new theater didn't fly, unfortunately. It would have been a great place to build a theater since it's in close proximity to Grosse Pointe and Bloomfield Hills (where my school Cranbrook is located) with lots of rich auto executive families like the Fords and Iaccocas to sponsor the arts. In its heyday, Detroit was akin to Chicago with great restaurants and beautiful places like The Fisher Theater. Rumor has it Detroit is on the rise again, and Janet and I couldn't be happier at the reinstatement of "little Paris."

*Silver-gray cocktail dress* with crepe dolman sleeves, crisscross boat neckline, and fitted bodice. Janet had worn this ingenious form-fitting number to a huge cocktail party where the women wore fabulous dresses, as was required in the day, and Janet wanted to outdo them! This was in Detroit at the Fisher Theatre and a lot of agents were there.

Janet caught a glance of movie star Edward Everett Horton lounging at the bar and dared by her partners in crime—of course, Chester and Fee Fee—went right over and talked to him and the other stars in the show *Oklahoma*, like Catherine Grayson and Gordon MacRea!

"Hello, darling! I'm so happy to see you and I haven't seen you in a long time!" Janet cozied right up to the group.

"Hello…" Edward politely turned around, stopped in his tracks, and had a look of recognition like a long lost friend. He said, "Darling, I haven't seen you in ages, you look ravishing!" He kissed her on the cheek, still a bit mystified as to who this new glam girl was.

Janet proceeded to introduce Edward to all her friends and all the stars of the show, heavens knows she was in familiar company. It was a plethora of "Darlings, you know this gorgeous creature, and that handsome devil…you were just fabulous, darling!"

Janet thought she'd have to get out of it quick because the jig would be up, so she left saying, "Our car is waiting, we must run! It was just fabulous seeing you, I will sleep well tonight! Toodle-loo, darling!" Schmoozing would never be the same!

*Avocado silk two-piece chiffon suit and matching pillbox hat (Jackie O style).* For this particular outfit, Mom took a millinery course and learned how to cover hats with that material, creating the beautiful avocado green silk pillbox hat to match the suit. Detroit, being the bustling metropolis it was in the '50s and '60s, had great restaurants and nightlife. She and her fellow models would lunch with auto executives like Henry Ford II and Henry Clay Ford as part of their job to impress notables in town. Mom admired the fact that Henry was good-looking and very polished, and both Fords seemed naturally impressed with her. Again the avocado suit ruled the day!

*Pink and yellow, A-line pregnancy sleeveless dress, simple boat line necklace.*

While there were glamorous occasions, there were some close calls with our little starlet, all dressed-to-kill. My parents' close friend, Ham, was the designated driver when the theater gang was party hopping. (He snapped took this shot of me, Mom and Dad in our living room when I was 10 years old.)

So Ham pulled out from a nightclub parking lot while talkative Janet was just getting into the car. And before you know it, he hit the gas. She only had one leg in and he zoomed off! "Ham!" the group of passengers cried desperately and he didn't stop! She had to hop about two blocks on one leg—a high-heeled leg, no less and finally, before he hit the main road, slammed on the breaks. Janet was four months pregnant with me and I may not have written this if Janet wasn't something of a Flying Wallenda. (But, I think we know that now...)

*Nancy Reagan-like long winter black pressed wool coat, with flaring bottom.*

The Rock House outside of Lexington, like The Little Inn, was one of the popular nightclubs and one of Janet's favorite college haunts. One night, Janet spread her coat out on a chair, and someone dropped a cigarette on it and it caught fire! Unbeknownst to the general public it had a Teflon lining, of all things. I guess it was the expectation that Janet would purchase it someday! With that beautiful coat burning, Janet resourcefully poured a pitcher of Martinis on it! Only a small part was singed so she was able to repair it in time for yet another Janet outing where she made it a point to first locate the fire extinguisher.

*Black cocktail dress, strapless, full skirt* – material was taffeta bodice with sheer chiffon cape scarf draping over the shoulder and around the skirt.

This is the historic little black number Janet wore to dance her way into my father's heart! Naturally, this was one of Janet's favorite designs, and definitely a key ensemble for me! I love how Janet danced on the tables with such joy and such a zeal for life *then* and *now*, at 83! Shake it, Janet! Shake it!

Absolutely, darling!